The Year of the Poet XII

September 2025

The Poetry Posse

inner child press, ltd.
'building bridges of cultural understanding'

The Poetry Posse 2025

Gail Weston Shazor
Shareef Abdur Rasheed
Teresa E. Gallion
hülya n. yılmaz
Noreen Snyder
Tzemin Ition Tsai
Elizabeth Esguerra Castillo
Jackie Davis Allen
Mutawaf Shaheed
Caroline 'Ceri' Nazareno
Ashok K. Bhargava
Alicja Maria Kuberska
Swapna Behera
Albert 'Infinite' Carrasco
Kimberly Burnham
Eliza Segiet
William S. Peters, Sr.

~ * ~

In order to maintain each poet's authentic voice, this volume has not undergone the scrutiny of editing. Please take time to indulge each contributor for their own creativity and aspirations to convey their uniqueness.

hülya n. yılmaz, Ph.D.
Director of Editing ~
Inner Child Press International

General Information

The Year of the Poet XII
September 2025 Edition

The Poetry Posse

1st Edition : 2025

This Publishing is protected under Copyright Law as a "Collection". All rights for all submissions are retained by the Individual Author and or Artist. No part of this Publishing may be Reproduced, Transferred in any manner without the prior **WRITTEN CONSENT** of the "Material Owners" or its Representative Inner Child Press. Any such violation infringes upon the Creative and Intellectual Property of the Owner pursuant to International and Federal Copyright Laws. Any queries pertaining to this "Collection" should be addressed to Publisher of Record.

Publisher Information
1st Edition : Inner Child Press
intouch@innerchildpress.com
www.innerchildpress.com

Copyright © 2025 : The Poetry Posse

ISBN-13 : 978-1-961498-72-3 (inner child press, ltd.)

$ 12.99

WHAT WOULD LIFE BE WITHOUT A LITTLE POETRY?

Dedication

This Book is dedicated to

Humanity, Peace & Poetry

the Power of the Pen

can effectuate change!

&

The Poetry Posse

past, present & future,

our Patrons and Readers &

the Spirit of our Everlasting Muse

*In the darkness of my life
I heard the music
I danced…
and the Light appeared
and I dance*

Janet P. Caldwell

Table of Contents

Foreword ix

Preface xiii

Emotions xv

Isolation ~ Empowerment ~ Confusion

The Poetry Posse

Gail Weston Shazor	1
Alicja Maria Kuberska	9
Jackie Davis Allen	15
Tzemin Ition Tsai	21
Noreen Snyder	27
Elizabeth Esguerra Castillo	33
Mutawaf Shaheed	39
hülya n. yılmaz	47
Teresa E. Gallion	53
Ashok K. Bhargava	59
Caroline Nazareno-Gabis	65
Swapna Behera	71

Table of Contents . . . *continued*

Albert Carassco	77
Kimberly Burnham	81
Eliza Segiet	89
William S. Peters, Sr.	95

Septmber's Featured Poets — 105

Abeera Mirza	107
Shaswata Gangopadhyay	113
Shahid Abbas Shahid	119
Snežana Šolkotović	125

Inner Child Press News — 133

Other Anthological Works — 179

Foreword

Isolation ~ Empowerment ~ Confusion

Emotions affect our mindset because it triggers same parts of the brain that used for decision making and problem solving.

Emotions are deeply interwoven elements of the human experience, often blending and shifting in response to internal conditions and external circumstances. Among these, isolation, empowerment, and confusion stand out as powerful yet seemingly contrasting emotions. While they may appear distinct, they are intricately connected and can influence each other in complex and sometimes unexpected ways.

Isolation is often characterized by a feeling of disconnection—whether physical, emotional, or social. It can be voluntary or involuntary and may result from events such as moving to a new place, losing a relationship, or simply feeling misunderstood. Isolation can lead to introspection, forcing individuals to confront their own thoughts and beliefs without external influence. While it is often associated with loneliness or sadness, isolation is not inherently negative; it can be a space for growth and clarity.

Confusion frequently accompanies isolation. Without the grounding presence of others or familiar environments, a person might struggle to understand their emotions or make decisions. Confusion arises when one's internal compass feels disrupted—when expectations no longer align with reality, or when identity feels uncertain. This disorientation can be distressing, but it also presents an opportunity to question assumptions and re-evaluate values.

From this space of isolation and confusion, the possibility of empowerment can emerge. Empowerment often begins with reclaiming a sense of control or understanding. It may stem from enduring and navigating through difficult emotional landscapes. As individuals confront their confusion and learn to be comfortable in solitude, they may discover inner strength and resilience. They begin to trust their intuition, make independent choices, and define their identities on their own terms.

Interestingly, empowerment does not always mean the absence of isolation or confusion. In fact, it often requires moving through these emotions with awareness. The journey from confusion to clarity, or from isolation to connection (even if only with oneself), can foster a deep and lasting sense of personal power. This dynamic interplay suggests that these emotions are not fixed endpoints, but stages in emotional growth.

In sum, isolation, confusion, and empowerment are deeply related emotional experiences. While isolation and confusion may be uncomfortable, they can serve as catalysts for self-discovery and empowerment. Understanding the relationship between them helps us see emotional struggle not as weakness, but as a pathway to strength and personal transformation.

Ashok K. Bhargava
President, Writers International Network, Canada

Coming Soon
www.innerchildpress.com

Preface

We, **Inner Child Press International, The Year of the Poet** and **The Poetry Posse** welcome you.

As we now are in our 12th year of monthly publications for **The Year of the Poet**, we continue to be excited.

This particular year we have chosen to feature a collection of human emotions. We do hope you enjoy the poet's perspectives on these subjects. Read ~ Learn.

For those of you who are not familiar with our story, back in 2013, a few of us poets got together with the simple intention of producing a book a month. That was our challenge. Since that time the enterprise has blossomed and brought forth a fruit that seems to keep on growing as evidenced as we enter 2023.

Our purpose is simple. Through our lyrical words and verse, we not only wish to share our poetic works, but we also have the poetic naiveté to believe that we can assist in the growth of consciousness of the things that have an effect our collective humanity. Therefore, we welcome your readership. For more about what we are attempting to accomplish, have a look at our Publishing Web Site . . . www.innerchildpress.com. If you would like to

know a bit more about this particular endeavor please stop by for a visit at :
www.innerchildpress.com/the-year-of-the-poet

Over the years, Inner Child Press has been socially active to bring awareness and catalog through literature the things that have an impact upon our world and its inhabitants. We have solicited, produced, underwritten and published quite a few volumes to that end. For more insight you may wish to visit : www.innerchildpress.com/the-anthology-market. If you are a writer, poet, or activist, you would be advised to keep a eye out for upcoming volumes should you desire to participate. All readers are welcomed as well. Note, that there is a myriad of published volumes that are available as a FREE PDF download as well as available for purchase at affordable prices.

We at this time extend to you our well wishes for your own personal journey and hope that you consider including us as a travel companion.

Bless Up

Bill

William S. Peters, Sr.

Publisher
Inner Child Press International
www.innerchildpress.com

Isolation ~ Empowerment ~ Confusion

Water Violet   Sunflower   Pink Larkspur

Isolation - A deeper sense of disconnection from others.
Empowerment - Gaining control over one's life.
Confusion - Navigating uncertainty and complexity.

This month with the themes covering "Isolation" (a deeper sense of disconnection from others), "Empowerment" (gaining control over one's life), and "Confusion" (navigating uncertainty and complexity), I was struck by a line from Rosemerry Wahtola Trommer's poem Belonging, which opens with, "And if it's true we are alone, we are alone together, the way blades of grass are alone, but exist as a field."

There are eight billion of us on this planet, where we have not yet learned how to connect deeply, love our neighbors, and feel safe in the complexity of the world. But we are here together whether we realize it or not, all of our fates are entangled in a jumble of shared resources: the water we drink, the plants we eat and make clothing and shelters from. In today's world who can grow all their own food, build their own house and car then drill for gasoline, refine it, and even if we have an electric car, who can build a solar panel and wire it to a vehicle so that we can travel or bring in resources that we need. And even if we could do all those things, who would want to sleep alone in their house and eat dinner alone.

Like it or not we are all in this world together like the blades of grass it might seem like we are alone, individual, growing ourselves but we rely on a myriad of others. The poets this month talk about our connections to life and to each other. Perhaps, you will find something in this volume that connects you more deeply to your own life.

In the words of Jacqueline Suskin "Poetry enables and empowers you to:
Find new ways to articulate and express yourself
Process emotional pain and heartache
Know yourself in a new, deep, and meaningful way
Express love, awe, and affection
Enhance self-awareness and critical thinking skills
Develop empathy, compassion, and insight
Celebrate life's moments and milestones
In other words, writing poetry is good for you!"

These poems from the Inner Child Press Poetry Posse will inspire you to find your own poetry and purpose.

Kimberly Burnham, PhD
(Integrative Medicine)
September, 2025 Spokane, WA & Portland, OR

Poets . . .
sowing seeds in the
Conscious Garden of Life,
that those who have yet to come
may enjoy the Flowers.

Poets, Writers . . . know that we are the enchanting magicians that nourishes the seeds of dreams and thoughts . . . it is our words that entice the hearts and minds of others to believe there is something grand about the possibilities that life has to offer and our words tease it forth into action . . . for you are the Poet, the Writer to whom the Gift of Words has been entrusted . . .

~ wsp

Poetry succeeds where instruction fails.

~ wsp

Open for Submissions

October 1st until December 31st

worldhealingworldpeace@gmail.com

Gail Weston Shazor

Gail Weston Shazor

Gail Weston Shazor is a lover of words. She is fond of the arcane, unusual and the not yet words.

Coining words at an early age, there was often a bit of trouble with teachers, but she always had her mother and aunt to back up her choices in expression. Born in Mississippi, she spent her early years with her grandparents. Each of the four left very careful influences on her pre-schooling. She learned in turn how women worked in and out of the home and how men worked in and out of the home to support the family. She learned that a lack of proper schooling was not the only way to learn and understanding life was a great teacher. As in most rural families of color, women had a greater chance of formal learning. Both of Gail's grandmothers read out loud to the family whether it was the bible or the newspapers and important documents to their spouses.

Gail Weston Shazor has authored (so far) Notes from the Blue Roof, A Overstanding of an Imperfect Love, HeartSongs and Lies My Grandfather's Told Me. The number of anthologies is too many to list with the premier accomplishment of one of the contributors to The Year of The Poet. Gail will always lend her ink to community projects and will purchase the books of fellow poets in the Inner Child Press family.

WIP

Say he just wants to be heard
I do too
Not that I think it matters much
This being heard thing
Mountains never moved because
I said I had anything to say
Nor minds changed
It's been in truth
Just the opposite
If I open my heart and spill
It makes no difference
To the fates
For they don't hear me either
I can scream it and
It is only my smallness that is seen
So I now wonder
If it's worth forming an opinion
At all
It is probably better to move
Along with crests and waves and currents
To be one with water again
And not fight against tides
To be taken under
Until I cannot breathe
To be at peace with who
What I am in the grander scheme
Of love and life
I think I might see if
I can barter breasts for a penis
And be truly one of the guys
By fashioning
And not simply by default

I could merge my sole into those
That truly have sway in this world
Because it seems I cannot
Be the one that is chosen

Just Me

I lost the title in my thoughts
So jumbled together as they were
Fleeting around the edges
Of memories, old, new and coming
Gone are the days
That we separated each other
By skin color
And when my generation dies
You will have to find colorism in a book
There is no forbidden love
No love that we have to be jailed for possessing
I can remember being bi-colored
High Yellow
Mullato
Mixed Race
And I only think on bears now
Would I fear a polar bear more than a brown bear?
Are my white relatives to be feared
More than my black or
My Indian tribe,
I don't think so
I wonder if sisters on each side
Of the Berlin Wall would genetically change
To enemies
Or did the Tutsis gain education because
They favored the Belgians more in complexion
Than the Hutus
All sharing a common language
For thousands of years with the TWA people
Why is a house slave better
Then a yard slave
Or a field slave

800,000 rumors on African soil
1 little girl on Mississippi soil
Who has never seen a bear free
Taught that life labeled dangerous
Had to be caged
And still clinging to the thought
Of Native ancestors that all life
Is cherished life
I drink water now
And ponder on the life that calls to me
From the margins
Jumbled together as they are
Whispering to be heard
This started as a Happy Mother's day piece
And so it goes
All women are wisdom bearers
And they exist to share the knowledge
Whether actively birthing or not
As they teach the children
All children
To see life
Question life
And protect life
So bears can continue to exist
Free
So we can continue to exist
Without labels
Free

Wristwatch

Hopeful
Here
I am though
Lost remain
Faded ribbons
Black on navy
Lost you with life
Shelves dusty on
Gifts kept
Life tuned in itself
Sadness of passing
Keep creep time
~Wristwatch~
Time creep keep
Passing of sadness
Itself in tuned life
Kept gifts
On dusty shelves
Life with you lost
Navy on black
Ribbons faded
Remain lost
Though i am
Here
Hopeful

Alicja Maria Kuberska

Alicja Maria Kuberska

Alicja Maria Kuberska – awarded Polish poetess, novelist, journalist, editor.

She is a member of the Polish Writers Associations in Warsaw, Poland and IWA Bogdani, Albania. She is also a member of directors' board of Soflay Literature Foundation, Our Poetry Archive (India) and Cultural Ambassador for Poland (Inner Child Press, USA)

Her poems have been published in numerous anthologies and magazines in : Poland, Czech Republic, Slovakia, Hungary,Ukraina, Belgium, Bulgaria, Albania, Spain, the UK, Italy, the USA, Canada, the UK, Argentina, Chile, Peru, Israel, Turkey, India, Uzbekistan, South Korea, Taiwan, China, Australia, South Africa, Zambia, Nigeria

She received two medals - the Nosside UNESCO Competition in Italy (2015) and European Academy of Science Arts and Letters in France (2017). Ahe also received a reward of international literary competition in Italy „ Tra le parole e 'elfinito" (2018). She was announced a poet of the 2017 year by Soflay Literature Foundation (2018).She also received : Bolesław Prus Prize Poland (2019), Culture Animator Poland (2019) and first prize Premio Internazionale di Poesia Poseidonia- Paestrum Italy (2019).

Isolation

My world is frozen in the past.
I take delight in old photos and films,
amazed at their timeless elegance,
and I wonder—what has become of us?
Where have the graceful women gone,
with flawless hair and dresses of beauty?
Who remembers the gentlemen in tails?
Does courtesy still exist at all?
A new time—wealthy and convenient.
New people—selfish and cruel.
A new world—without rules, without empathy.
A new me—enclosed in a white rose.

Awakening

I fall silent, sink into stillness, drown.
I vanish like Ophelia in the lake's dark waters.
Above me, noiselessly passing,
night and day ignite and fade,
stars are kindled, then extinguished,
clouds lean into the mirror of the water,
while in my hushed world
schools of shimmering fish drift by,
and delicate plants sway beneath the surface.
Above me—summer storms, winter blizzards,
the wind breaks branches, reeds are whispering,
birds are singing, insects hum,
and I, wrapped in silence, remain unmoving.
I will wait a moment, to be reborn,
to tear apart the cocoon,
and like a mayfly rise above the tranquil waters.

Forest

The green pierces through me.
I touch the rough bark of pines,
I lean against the whiteness of birches.
Carpets of moss yield beneath my steps.
The air is heavy with dampness.
I free my thoughts from the cacophony of emotions,
the inner rift begins to heal.
Peace drips like resin, sealing the wounds.
I regain freedom and independence.
I lift my eyes toward the sky.
I am in the world's greatest cathedral.
The trunks of mighty trees, like columns,
hold aloft a ceiling carved of clouds.
Chandeliers of stars fade and flare,
and at dawn the sun gleams like a drop of gold.
The wind, hidden in the rustle of leaves and grass,
hums its hymn of freedom.
Birds join in, singing loudly.
The music seeps into the air—
dew drops tremble like notes.

Jackie Davis Allen

Jackie Davis Allen

Jackie Davis Allen, otherwise known as Jacqueline D. Allen or Jackie Allen, grew up in the Cumberland Mountains of Appalachia. As the next eldest daughter of a coal miner father and a stay at home mother, she was the first in her family to attend and graduate from college. Her siblings, in their own right, are accomplished, though she is the only one, to date, that has discovered the gift of writing.

Graduating from Radford University, with a Bachelor's of Science degree in Early Education, she taught in both public and private schools. For over a decade she taught private art classes to children both in her home and at a local Art and Framing Shop where she also sold her original soft sculptured Victorian dolls and original christening gowns.

She resides in northern Virginia with her husband, taking much needed get-aways to their mountain home near the Blue Ridge Mountains, a place that evokes memories of days spent growing up in the Appalachian Mountains.

A lover of hats, she has worn many. Following marriage to her college sweetheart, and as wife, mother, grandmother, teacher, tutor, artist, writer, poet and crafter, she is a lover of art and antiques, surrounding herself, always, with books, seeking to learn more.

In 2015 she authored *Looking for Rainbows, Poetry, Prose and Art*, and in 2017, *Dark Side of the Moon*. Both books of mostly narrative poetry were published by Inner Child Press and were edited by hulya n. yilmaz in 2019, *No Illusions. Through the Looking Glass*, which was nominated to be considered for a Pulitzer Prize by the publisher and editor of Inner Child Press, ltd.

http://www.innerchildpress.com/jackie-davis-allen.php
jackiedavisallen.com

Isolation

Hospitalized, for nearly a year, aching,
from a ruptured appendix, in pain,
My life has been interrupted.

No third grade for me. No time
With my classmates. However,
I'm given a 50-50 chance to survive.

Swollen up like a balloon, I'm assaulted
with intravenous infusions. A straight
jacket removed allows some freedom.

Months later, offered a private room,
I prefer my pregnant roommates, who pay
well, for my forays to the vending machines.

I know that "private room" is where
they put people that are going to die.
I saw the velvet drapes yesterday.

I saw the stretcher rolling down the hall
I saw the undertaker, the parents.
I heard them crying, wailing.

I'm sorry, sad for them.
But I'm not going to die!
Give that room to somebody else!

Empowerment

My piggy bank groans.
It smiles its thanks. Tips its hat.
My tummy aches. I'm not going home.

My kidneys are failing, day and night.
I struggle to exert any kind of control.
And still, the nurses deliver medication.

I hate those hypodermic needles!
I know! I'll hide! Behind the door,
beneath the bed. Alas, I've been found.

There's a restroom in the waiting room!
It's got a door with a lock! Now, I'm safe!
I wait. I try to hold my breath.

Oh no! I hear keys rattling! Suddenly,
A maintenance man is staring at me!
And a nurse! She ushers me back to bed.

I've no say in anything. I hurt. I'm angry.
I miss my family. I'm lonesome Even still,
my mind keeps me busy, wondering.

Jackie Davis Allen

Confusion Resolved

I'm eight years old.
A semi-permanent resident,
I'm supposed to be recovering.

I'm in a wheelchair, coming down the elevator,
guided, deposited into a semi-private room.
Far away from my bed. In the maternity ward.

Why the maternity ward?
A curious child, bent upon adventure,
Someone thought I needed supervision?

I'm finally sharing a room with a little girl.
In the adjacent bed, this blond-headed
intrusion has brought me a gift. Head lice!

She's discharged. My possessions, destroyed!
The head lice are finally no more. Confused,
I scratch my head. I've a new roommate!

It's my mother! She's pregnant.
But I don't know that.
Only that she has a big belly.

Am I dreaming? Surely not!
By my bed, a nurse rouses me, "Let's go.
Here's your robe. You have a new baby sister!"

Up the elevator, still half asleep, confused,
We arrive. Before me, I see two babies.
One in either arm. "Which do you want?"

I choose one, correctly. (The other is a boy.)
They meet. Fall in love. They marry.
Still together more than a half-century later.

Tzemin Ition Tsai

Noreen Snyder

Dr. Tzemin Ition Tsai comes from the Republic of China(Taiwan). In addition to being a professor of literature at a university, he is more committed to writing poems, novels, and proses. He is also an editor of "Reading, Writing and Teaching" academic text, an International editor of "Contemporary dialogues" literary periodical in Macedonia, and Vice-Chairman of the International Jury of the SAHITTO INTERNATIONAL AWARD in Bangladesh, and a columnist for "Chinese Language Monthly" in Taiwan.

In a wide range of literary creations, he is particularly fond of interesting stories or novels, and writing articles or poems about the feelings of nature and human beings. He has won many national literary awards. His literary works have been anthologized and published in books, journals, and newspapers in more than 55 countries and have been translated into more than 24 languages.

Noreen Snyder

The Lone Lantern in the Fog

The fog,
older than the island itself,
with pallid breath,
swallows both shorelines and sorrows whole.
A lantern shivers,
a stranded star in exile,
its flame a frail heartbeat
between the tide's abyss
and the silence of the night.

Darkness,
An untitled elegy, soldiers stand like torn fragments of scripture,
dialects dissolve in damp air,
becoming solitary echoes
of a language unloved.
Who remembers?
Who follows?
This lantern is no beacon for ships,
but a stubborn ember declaring,
in the vast, indifferent cosmos.
Isolation, too, can carve its way
into eternity.

Rusty Bridge In The Harbor

Rust blooms
in the creases of palms,
red as wounds,
yet gleaming with the salt-lit sheen of toil.
Each flake of iron
a miniature star,
forged from sweat,
burning quiet constellations of labor.

This harbor,
cranes bend like mythic, weary beasts,
their arms grinding against wind and sea.
Containers rise like mute mountains,
cold monoliths
made to tremble only
by the coarse chorus of human voices.

The workers' throats,
hoarse as broken steel,
resound deeper than sirens,
strike harder than tides
upon the rock of time.
We are not rust.
We are the furnace's last flame
from burning and breaking.

Noreen Snyder

The Old Stairways, Whose Direction?

Steps upon steps,
unanswered riddles of time,
damp as the veins of abandoned mines,
glistening with the patina of dusk.
Alleys,
a labyrinth hand-carved by history,
twisting like dislocated memory.
One path ascends to dawn's promise,
another slips into the cavernous unknown.
Direction?
Teahouse smoke whispers upward,
lanterns sway with false certainties.
Travelers chase silhouettes of light,
yet in the cracks of stone,
a deeper voice reverberates.
Is this ascent
a journey home,
or an exile from the self?
Old stairways
become gravestones of existence.
With every step, confusion
etches itself deeper
into the soul's stone.

Noreen Snyder

Noreen Snyder

Noreen Ann Snyder has been writing since she was a teenager. She writes a variety of different topics. Her favorite poetic forms are Sonnets, Blitz, Haiku, Tanka, and Free Verse. She always learning different poetic forms.

Noreen Ann Snyder is a poet, writer, and an author of five books, (four books are co-authored with her late husband, Garry A. Snyder.) Her poetry is in several Inner Child Press Anthologies. She is the founder of The Poetry Club on Facebook.

Noreen Snyder

On Empowerment

At one time I didn't use to be this way.
I used to be soundless as a shadow
still as a frozen pond.
Now I learned to speak up
no longer afraid
Look at me!   Now you can't shut me up
for speaking the truth, being honest.
Sometimes I do talked too much.
But I want to be the voice
for the voiceless. I have something to say.
I want to educate them not to be fearful.
It's okay. Take your time.
Then before you know it
you're no longer nonvocal
you are just like me.

Be United

Let's join hands and be

united as one big fam.

We are all human.

Noreen Snyder

Moved On

I have moved on
after six and a half years
but still no one can replace you.
You're always in my memories,
in my mind, in my thoughts.
What can I say that
I haven't said already?
I know I will see you again.
I am waiting for that day.
That put a smile on my face.
Our love is here for eternity.
I never thought I say these words
I learned to live without you
and I don't want to but I have.

Elizabeth E. Castillo

Elizabeth Esguerra Castillo

Elizabeth Esguerra Castillo is a multi-awarded and an Internationally-Published Contemporary Author/Poet and a Professional Writer / Creative Writer / Feature Writer / Journalist / Travel Writer from the Philippines. She has 2 published books, "Seasons of Emotions" (UK) and "Inner Reflections of the Muse", (USA). Elizabeth is also a co-author to more than 60 international anthologies in the USA, Canada, UK, Romania, India. She is a Contributing Editor of Inner Child Magazine, USA and an Advisory Board Member of Reflection Magazine, an international literary magazine. She is a member of the American Authors Association (AAA) and PEN International.

Web links:

Facebook Fan Page

https://free.facebook.com/ElizabethEsguerraCastillo

Google Plus

https://plus.google.com/u/0/+ElizabethCastillo

Elizabeth Esguerra Castillo

Rise after the Storm

I rise from the ashes of forgotten days,
veins humming with fire older than time.
The universe whispers my name
through constellations no one else can read,
reminding me
that I am both the spark and the flame,
both the seeker and the path.

Mountains bend to the weight of my will, oceans echo the
cadence of my breath.
What once was silence within me has become a chorus of
thunder,
and the ground trembles
not with fear,
but with recognition.

I am the storm
and the stillness after— a living testament
that nothing broken
remains shattered forever.

Exile of Silence

A glass veil hangs between me and the living world.
I see their gestures,
hear the muted   laughter— but sound dissolves
before it reaches my skin.

I sit with shadows
who speak in ancient riddles, their voices soft as candle smoke,
curling into my solitude.
The moon becomes my confidant, patient, silver-eyed,
watching the hollow hours stretch into eternity.

Yet in this exile of silence, I find a strange sanctuary— a still pool where
the cosmos lowers her face, and I finally see
my own reflection in the stars.

Eternal Dusk

The path splits— not in two,
but in a thousand shimmering directions, each one alive,
each one trembling with possibility.

The air itself is liquid, bending time, fracturing meaning.
Even my thoughts echo
like voices trapped in labyrinths, where questions multiply
faster than answers can breathe.

I reach for certainty—
but my hands close around smoke.
Every step becomes both departure and arrival, and I
wonder if confusion itself
is the language of the divine, a reminder that clarity
is but a fleeting lantern, flickering in the eternal dusk.

Mutawaf Shaheed

Mutawaf Shaheed

C. E. Shy has been writing since the seventh grade. He continued writing through high school, until he became more involved in sports. After his graduation, he worked at the White Motors Company where he wrote for the company's newspaper. He started a column called: "The Poet's Corner." That was his first published work.

www.innerchildpress.com/c-e-shy.php

Mutawaf Shaheed

All Day Long

Sitting, standing, even lying on my side,
trying to reside in that part of you that
made you forget us, we, me. Questions?
marked a spot where I forgot to tell you
how much you meant, mean to me, us ,we.

All day long, all that exists in me, us, we.
The last time you tried to cancel your trip
to destiny you wound here near, close to
me. It was closer than expected.

We never felt like this before you came,
then we came to terms that we wanted you
to keep coming back again. The table was
bare until you put something on it.

There is now, some one for my mind to dine
with. The dawn was gone before we knew
it and it took Coltrane with it.

The we in me, stays focused on us being able
to touch you with our, your vital signs, cause
like minds to feel alike.

The folks on the buses and trains, regain strength
being the ads that the TV plays. Busy, seeing who can
be the busiest, who can be the CEO of the low blow
company.

Spiritual felons on the run from themselves, can't
seem to escape the voices that make the demands,
that turn women into man's worst friend.

They can't help or hide them from the dog catchers.
Tethered to whether or not they should be with me,
we or us.? It's all the same when you get out the game.
There is only me, the we, and us belong to them, those
and theirs.

Havoc

What is supposed to make sense
makes a mess. Crooked ain't straight.
What's worthwhile to many bares no
fruit to others. A thousand zeros, is zero.

I never got a dime from the heaven you
designed. In fact, I caught hell trying to
get a penny.

The androids taking opioids gain fame from
the murder game killing kids is their favorite
ploy.

Rewarded with peanut butter and jelly for
their efforts. They will survive as long as
they can duck the bus their master drives.

They share nightmares with night time.
It's after sunset, in the dark they thrive.
Doing dirt in the dark saying its fertilizer
to help plastic plants stay alive.

Will they ever know that their creation, is
a perfect infection?

He's Okay!

Single jingles still mingle in my
head from time to time.
Every now and then I remember
the crimes committed by the
framers of the nursery rhymes.
As a kid nobody wanted to be the
Indians, because the cowboys and

Calvary always won.
We killed all the Indians and
the buffalo too.
Don't worry about that we have the
whole world to screw.
We'll find the enemy lurking in the
grass. They are watching us from
 behind the trees.

We can even find them in a cool
southern breeze.
The enemy is hiding in the clouds.
Waiting on Mars. Some of the enemies
are sneaking up on us from behind the sun.
If we can't find some we'll
make up one.

Just in case you forget, we got the
the Hollywood movies to back-up
our bets.
The TV stations are standing by, ready
and willing to support the lie.
We have all who listen
 beg for lies.

Mutawaf Shaheed

We are at a point now we don't
wear a disguise.
We have made stars out of serial killers.
Dracula is their cult hero.
We will call again on the Negro slave;
he will forgive us all the way to his grave.
Don't worry about him; he's okay.

hülya n. yılmaz

hülya n. yılmaz

Liberal Arts Professor Emerita, hülya n. yılmaz [sic] is Co-Chair and Director of Editing Services at Inner Child Press International, a published author, ghostwriter, and translator (EN, DE, and TU; in any direction). Her literary contributions appeared in a large number of national and international anthologies.

hülya writes creatively to attain and nourish a comprehensive awareness for and development of our humanity.

hülya n. yılmaz, a traveler on the journey called "life" . . .

Writing Web Site
https://hulyanyilmaz.com/

Editing Web Site
https://hulyasfreelancing.com

hülya n. yılmaz

how isolation feels like to me

you are on an open sea,
drifting farther away from the pin-sized land

on a self-made galley of fast-rotting planks
one hole chases another in a vicious race

only quicksand is at your disposal
but the vain attempt to fill the openings
is strong in you still

Alas!

the welded-in rod
is weighing you down,
desperately determined
to make out of you
a lifetime companion
to drown it repeatedly

on
its
rusty
hook
you dangle
on and on

a new i

missing you
not because of a need
or for a want

the yearning is different from before
neither acute nor painful, only aware
that the mirage of you
has its pillar no more

these days
fairy tales
fail to impress me

i finally woke up to a new day,
no longer missing you . . .
that is, your version i thought to be true

help me, Euterpe!

Euterpe, i beg of you
hear my plea
shield the natal passion,
the first resolve to forget
and the quest for a new breath,
the now and the here

inspire
my desire
to define
the divine

rid me of yesteryear,
free me from the confused self,
enable my soul to reject its cage,
sate my shadow's final plea,
let it soar in its primal roar,
prancing its essence in a trance

help me shape in clarity the newly dawning day!

Teresa E. Gallion

Teresa E. Gallion

Teresa E. Gallion is a seeker on a journey to work on unfolding spiritually in this present lifetime. Writing is a spiritual exercise for Teresa. Her passions are traveling the world and hiking the mountain and desert landscapes of the western United States. Her journeys into nature are nurtured by the Sufi poets Rumi and Hafiz. The land is sacred ground and her spiritual temple where she goes for quiet reflection and contemplation. She has published five books: Walking Sacred Ground, Contemplation in the High Desert, Chasing Light, a finalist in the 2013 New Mexico/Arizona Book Awards, Scent of Love, a finalist in the 2021 New Mexico/Arizona Book Awards and Come Egypt in 2024. She has two CDs, *On the Wings of the Wind* and *Poems from Chasing Light*. Her work has appeared in numerous journals and anthologies.

Website: http://teresagallion.yolasite.com/

Teresa E. Gallion

Shades of Isolation

Isolation is not a dirty word.
It is a clean shaven, two edge sword.
Bourne out of necessity
to create space for soul
to practice diligence
in its quest to grow.

Positive and negative energy
bump against the feet.
You must learn to walk
in the deep space of both
to develop the strength
to survive the coming storms.

Unshaken

Unshaken by the fall,
I hear the voice
that echoes from my soul.

An unyielding force pushes me
like a committed friend.
No judgment, only cheers in the background.

I was born to be independent.
Deeply drawn to the earth sphere.
My name is a power word.

I build castles in the sand
that bloom into my dreams.
The world is my playground.

When I whisper in the wind,
I hear my inner voice call my name.
Each murmur moves me forward.

Nothing can stop me
on my journey into enlightenment.
I get closer one step at a time.

Teresa E. Gallion

Ball of Confusion

A black velvet blanket
holds a billion lanterns
grazing in the night sky.

I find myself frozen in place.
A mind racing like shooting stars
asking, who are you?

That breath of air from my lungs.
That bead of water heating my face.
That fire burning in my chest.

The night silence makes me tremble
as the darkness plays jazz
to soothe my bones.

I do not understand
the air, the water, the fire
that races through my veins.

The message is a ball of confusion.
Rolling down my back
wet and burning in the night breeze.

There is something sacred
stirring in the night.
It feels like despair.

I need a curtain of light
to wrap around the darkness
crawling on the ground.

There is a call to prayer in darkness.
Filled with grace and light
for spirit knows where I belong.

Ashok K. Bhargava

Ashok K. Bhargava

Ashok Bhargava is a poet, writer, inspirational speaker and a literary consultant. He has attended poetry conferences in Italy, Turkey, India and Philippines. His latest book "Riding the Tide" about his battle with cancer has been translated and published in Arabic, Hindi, Telugu and Bengali languages. He is a contributing writer to several anthologies worldwide including World Poetry Almanac 2014. He has been published in numerous print and online magazines.

Ashok has won many accolades including Poet Ambassador to Japan, Kalidasa International award, World Poetry Lifetime Achievement award, Writers Beyond Borders Peace award and Tapsilog Leadership award for his community involvement. He is founder of Writers International Network Canada Society to discover, nourish, recognize and celebrate writers, poets and artists and to assist them to network with the community at large. He is the author of eight books of poetry and one anthology. He is Artist-in-Residence at Moberly Arts & Cultural Centre and also co-edits the literary section of The Link Newspaper.

Ashok K. Bhargava

In Confusion, I Wait

How much knowing is enough to be enlightened?
The more I read, the more I feel darkened.

Life is a riddle in a thin disguise,
I glue together parts of me just to survive.

If the soul is eternal, why do I feel I'm losing ground?
The more I seek, the less the truth is found.

Confused voices crash like waves in my head,
Some whisper hope, others fill me with dread.

What once felt sure now crumbles in doubt,
Each turn I take just turns me inside out.

Still, I learn to sit and stay,
To breathe, not solve, and wait the storm away.

Sometimes clarity is painfully slow to come,
A whispered truth… until thy will is done.

The Shape of Isolation

I did not want to. I wanted to become the earth,
Spinning in my own orbit, patiently.

But with limited choices,
We can't always become what we want.

We must hold on to whatever remains –
Ordinary moments, simple situations, even annoyances.

Your promise to reach out someday,
After severing all bonds, it never came.

A month then another, and then again.
I waited, silent, standing on the cliff.

I wanted to stay connected - not just a lone
Echo in an empty shell.

No knock, no step, no hand upon the door.
The clock ticks no more.

In this silence, I begin to find
That solitude can reshape an unfulfilled mind.

The Quiet Rising

I worked the soil with my bare hands,
Planting hope in quiet, broken lands.

The seeds became smiling blossoms bright,
Sunflowers glowing with golden light.

They shine like lamps through darkest skies,
Radiating truth where silence lies.

Defying odds, they shape the day,
Turning always toward the sun's brave way.

They do not know what it means to be
A light born of pain and tenacity —

A flame forged deep within the core
Of a heart that's been shattered before.

Yet here I stand, my spine unbent,
Fearless, bold, and eloquent.

No force can dim this fire within —
I rise. I roar. I burn. I win

Caroline 'Ceri Naz' Nazareno Gabis

Caroline 'Ceri' Nazareno-Gabis

Caroline 'Ceri Naz' Nazareno-Gabis, author of Velvet Passions of Calibrated Quarks, World Poetry Canada International Director to Philippines is a multi-awarded poet, editor, journalist, educator, peace and women's advocate. She believes that learning other's language and culture is a doorway to wisdom.

Among her poetic belts include **Gabrielle Galloni Memorial Panorama International Youth Award 2022**, Panorama Youth Literary Awards 2020, 7th Prize Winner in the 19th, 20th and 21^{St} Italian Award of Literary Festival; Writers International Network-Canada ''Amazing Poet 2015'', The Frang Bardhi Literary Prize 2014 (Albania), Poet Journalist Award 2014 (Tuzla, Istanbul, Turkey) and World Poetry Empowered Poet 2013 (Vancouver, Canada). She's a featured member of Association of Women's Rights and Development (AWID), The Poetry Posse, Galaktika Poetike, Asia Pacific Writers and Translators (APWT), Axlepino and Anacbanua. Her poetry and children's stories have been featured in different anthologies and magazines worldwide.

Links to her works:

http://panitikan.ph/2018/03/30/caroline-nazareno-gabis/

https://apwriters.org/author/ceri_naz/

http://www.aveviajera.org/nacionesunidasdelasletras/id1181.html

Caroline 'Ceri' Nazareno-Gabis

The Wallflower

She wears silence,
Unnoticed bud,
She stands soft and unknown,
Her shadows spin
In the stillness,
Like a quiet flame,
Eyes like a dusky moon,
In the hush of flares,
And dancing gentle games,
The petals are unseen,
The forgotten corners,
Where her name once tied,
Her face was there,
Collecting moments,
Not in isolation,
Just reminding you that,
Not all need a stage,
Not all flowers need sunlight,
Not all dancers need the spotlight,
Just a quiet wallflower,
A lone flower of twilight,
 The world has never heard yet,
Unstoppable bloom.

The Zeitgeist's Vow

The clamor of now
Whispers fabric of the ageless vows
Between revolutions
Truth that speaks the seeds of fortitude,
Even the world mirrors broken illusions,
Broken vows across the walls,
The soul needs a lifting spirit
To console and to support,
Which makes our hearts composed,
In the hums of distractions and wars,
The mindful taps one's shoulders
To dream with hopes and strength,
It is the breathing movement,
That pushes our leaps towards
The echoes of queer questions
That we carry deep.

Bedlam State

The world cracked the chaotic screams,
Like thunder and turbulence,
Our hearts are pressed against the cages
Souls searching for flights to keep control.
Kindness roars to forget the pain
Like children weeps in algorithmic raindrops,
While poets write their deepest thoughts
To pour down mercy and calm,
We ache with hands that mend
Through prayers and verses,
So let the confusion write its labeled doom,
 Face it unshattered, brave the storm.

Swapna Behera

Swapna Behera

Swapna Behera is a trilingual poet, translator, environmentalist, editor from India and author of seven books of different genres including one on children's literature on Environment. She is the recipient of International UGADI AWARD 2019, honoured from Gujurat Sahitya Akademi 2022, 2021 International Poesis Award of Honor as Jury, Pentasi B World Fellow Poet, Honoured Poet of India from Seychelles Government and International awards from Algeria, Morocco, Kajhakhstan, modern Arabic Literary Renaissance of Egypt, International Arts Council Argentina etc. Her stories, poems, articles are published in many International and National magazines and ezines. Her poem A NIGHT IN THE REFUGEE CAMP is translated into 67 languages. She has received over 60 National and International Awards. At present she is the Cultural Ambassador for India and South Asia of Inner Child and the life member of Odisha Environmental Society

Email
swapna.behera@gmail.com

Web Site
http://swapnabehera.in/

if my shadow forgets me

yes,
if my shadow forgets me
I may be alone in the crowd
but a lamp post always stands alone
my solitude has a bulging wallet
at times I write the song of my legacy
I canvas my dreams
my pathos, my victory
beneath the galaxy
I stand as a lonely gospel
my designation, desolation,
profound loneliness
is the celebration of seventh season
I can float in the
perilous cloud
as a polar star
my tricky self will come out of the cage
in search of my own freedom
years will melt
lonely islands will echo
a bird will fly from my skeleton
tears will dilute my fear
to reflect a new Sun
the heart will create a new estuary

one to one talk with empowerment

Swapna: greetings from India respected
Empowerment: yes namaste
S: How are you?
E: I am superb, thank you.
S: please define yourself
E: I am the justice within. I flow as a river,
 glow as the virgin eyes of a new baby
S: But you are invisible
E; yes, I am but can't you feel me?
S: umm
E: I am certainly there
when you have a control over your vices you feel the vibration
when you have the ethical fight against socioeconomic injustice
when you speak for the depressed and downtrodden
when you create a new language for the birds, animals and trees
when you sing the welcome song for the new generation
when you dance for the cancer patients and dyslexia
when you are humble to learn
when you reason and listen to the tears
when you take social responsibilities
when you have the inner strength to forgive
when you heal your own emotional wounds
when you can sacrifice and create your own aura
when your pain is converted into power
when you stand for truth and only for Truth
I am there
S: Any message you wish to spread to the world
E: "Your existence is your empowerment."
Swapna: thanks a lot. we will meet soon
Empowerment: good luck Swapna

confusion vs fusion

confusion is not the conclusion
it is a blurred decision
a collaboration
with my heart
to understand my effusion
that takes a coronation
 to be my declaration

fusion is the axiom
love dances in tandem
mingling makes twinkling
 a multilayer inclusion
when musing ooze out all confusions
lo! behold a flag furls at the horizon
Adam has the confusion
but Newton has the fusion
by the way
I love apples ….

Albert 'Infinite' Carrasco

Albert 'Infinite' Carassco

Albert "Infinite The Poet" Carrasco is an urban poet, mentor and public speaker.

Albert believes his experience of growing up in poverty, dealing with drugs and witnessing murder over and over were lessons learnt, in order to gain knowledge to teach. Albert's harsh reality and honesty is a powerfully packed punch delivered through rhyme. Infinite grew up in the east part of the Bronx and still resides there, so he knows many young men will follow the same dark path he followed looking for change. The life of crime should never be an option to being poor but it is, very often.

Infinite poetry @lulu.com

Alcarrasco2 on YouTube

Infinite the poet on reverbnation

Infinite Poetry

www.lulu.com/us/en/shop/al-infinite-carrasco/infinite-poetry/paperback/product-21040240.html

www.innerchildpress.com/albert-carrasco

Isolation empowerment confusion

I grew up in hard times, silver spoons weren't the utensils we used as we dined, plastic and rusted aluminum utensils worked fine. The community i lived in lived with the same conditions,

Struggle meals were always on rotation as we lived on a struggle income. We prayed our government assisted checks would come on the first without delay to end hunger and thirst in the months final days. To the outside world, our poverish oppression and tradition of always having "less than" put us in a state of isolation. We had monetary borders, we couldn't go to a restaurant and get the pleasure of having a waiter take our orders because we knew we couldn't pay for those orders when the meal was over. When we walked through clothing stores we were watched for theft because they wanted to make sure we left with the same items we wore and nothing more because we "looked" poor, on the lucky days when we got to actually buy something security was definitely going to stop us and match merch and receipts before we could walk out the door. My birth was significant in breaking the generational curse of being dependent on rationing food first to first, had to get my family out this environment. I was born with that empowerment. Years later my family was able to interior decorate our apartment, we no longer needed the government for food or rent, I kept my thoughts free of mental pollution and captivity thinking what once was will always be, I am the solution to end ... stagnated confusion.

Kimberly Burnham

Kimberly Burnham

A brain health expert (PhD in Integrative Medicine) and award-winning poet, Kimberly Burnham lives with her wife and family in Spokane, Washington. Kim speaks extensively on peace, brain health, and "*Awakenings: Peace Dictionary, Language and the Mind, a Daily Brain Health Program.*" She recently published "*Heschel and King Marching to Montgomery A Jewish Guide to Judeo-Tamarian Imagery.*" Currently work includes "*Call and Response To Maya Stein an Anthology of Wild Writing*" and a how-to non-fiction book, "*Using Ekphrastic Fiction Writing and Poetry to Create Interest and Promote Artists, Writers, and Poets.*"

Follow her at https://amzn.to/4fcWnRB

Kimberly Burnham

Pathiception

In Rosemerry Wahtola Trommer's poem Seeking Purpose
she quotes Orison Swett Marden, "The golden opportunity
you are seeking is in yourself
It is not in your environment
it is not in luck or chance …"

Trommer goes on to say, "some days
a woman wishes the world would
just tell her, her purpose …"

Sometimes when we are listening
we can hear ourselves growing towards our purpose
in medicine we talk about proprioception
that internal sense of where your body is in space
how you know how to touch the tip of your nose
with your eyes closed
or how to lift your foot at a curb without looking down
that sense of where you and your joints are in your
environment
in the universe

Perhaps there is a word like pathiception
or trailing conjuring the image of a dog
smelling for the direction they must go
a word long since forgotten
that means the sense of growing and moving
along your path
a sense of knowing where you are in relationship
to your goals
the steps you must take driven by an internal sense
of where you are going

An inner knowing whether you are doing
what you are meant to do
or be
in this world
without anyone telling you
you just know this is the poem you are meant to write
this is the story you are meant to live
a guide to yourself and others
on the path

Good For You

Writing poetry is good medicine.
at least, it is for me
that small lift of joy
as I begin to listen
to myself

Even when I'm not writing
I'm quietly leaning toward it
considering the red of last night's sky
the way the August grass crumbles under foot
like dry gluten-free bread

Poetry lets me step
just outside my own body
and watch for a moment

How did I really feel
after that bowl of steaming pho,
tofu floating like light brown sea lions
in a warm sea

I turn the moment over
in the soft light of memory
and notice how the waiter
silently handed me the menus
motioned to the tables
as though I worked there

I found a place for my family
passed the menus around
like offerings promising deliciousness

Now I sit at home
with my laptop
my belly full
the cold brush of the air conditioner
against my left leg near the window
a small reminder I am lucky
to have this room
this machine
and above all
precious time

It is quiet
three dogs and a fourth visitor roam the back yard
one child watches a movie behind a closed door
another flies toward a new life at college
one moves with strength in a jujitsu match
one shops with her mother

Everyone accounted for
everyone finding their path to becoming
exactly who they are meant to be

And so I write
grateful and steady
watching the complexity of my life
open like a jewel box
in the early afternoon

The Basketball

Let it go
the ball has already slipped
over the painted line
a small orange sphere rolling
into someone else's hands

Yes they scored
Yes your heart tightened

But look
the court still opens before you
like a wide bright canvas
your hands healthy
the air is still waiting
to carry your next pass

The past already vanishing
into the echo of soles on hardwood.
only this moment
breathes beneath your feet

So run
as if you have never missed
as if every heartbeat
were the precious

Play as though
mistake is just another word
for beginning
again with wisdom learned
self-forgiveness will sharpen your aim

Eliza Segiet

Eliza Segiet

Eliza Segiet graduated with a Master's Degree in Philosophy at Jagiellonian University.

Received *Global Literature Guardian Award* – from Motivational Strips, World Nations Writers Union and Union Hispanomundial De Escritores (UHE) 2018.

Nominated for the Pushcart Prize 2019, 2021.

Laureate *Naji Naaman Literary Prize 2020,*

International Award Paragon of Hope (2020),

World Award 2020 *Cesar Vallejo* for Literary Excellence. Laureate of the Special Jury *Sahitto International Award* 2021, World Award *Premiul Fănuș Neagu* 2021.

Finalist *Golden Aster Book* World Literary Prize 2020, *Mili Dueli* 2022, Voci nel deserto 2022.

At the international Festival of Poetry CAMPIONATO MONDIALE DI POESIA (2021/2022) she won the title of vice-champion of the world.

Award BHARAT RATNA RABINDRANATH TAGORE INTERNATIONAL AWARD (2022).

Award - *World Poets Association* (2023).

Laureate Between words and infinity *"International Literary Award (2023).*

Scoundrel

Before, he thought
that this ordinary rainy day
would change nothing in his life.
But when he opened the envelope,
uncertainty passed through him.
He read:
Please report for further tests.
A bolt of despair pierced his body.

On the planet of loneliness,
in a place
where he constantly encountered only:
silence, peace, and rain,
he waited for the diagnosis.

Surrounded by silence, without
 – support,
 – care,
 – interest.

"*I'll defeat you, scoundrel!*" – he shouted.

He succeeded.
Wiser than before, he knows
that life has been granted to him again.
And *friends* – it's just a word!

The seasons have power
 – they are reborn.
A man has one road
 – toward death.
The faithful ones can be found
 – but it's an art of choice.

Translated by Dorota Stępińska

The Cloak of Truth

In the kingdom of belief in friendship,
she got lost.
She found her way
when the cloak of truth came down.
It revealed predatory instincts,
the desire to tear from her
the control over her own life.
Kindness,
built on pretence,
slowly
began to loosen its grip.

She began to have her own opinion,
her own voice.
She no longer cared
how she should act,
the false counsel
ceased to work.
Drawn closer to the truth,
she moved farther and farther away.
She was guided only
by her own feeling.

Translated by Dorota Stępińska

Eliza Segiet

The Spring of Solitude

When she sat on the bench in a park,
she wasn't sure if he would come.

How do you recognize someone
you met on the Internet?
He could have a fake photo.
And why, on a beautiful August day,
would he hold an umbrella in his hand?
Her blue eyes
looked left, then right.
Mothers strolling with children
made her smile.
Apparently, men
don't like parks.
Or maybe they don't like children?

Cracked dreams showed
that the spring of solitude
would be hers forever.

Translated by Dorota Stępińska

William S. Peters Sr.

William S. Peters, Sr.

Bill's writing career spans a period of well over 50 years. Being first Published in 1972, Bill has since went on to Author in excess of 50+ additional Volumes of Poetry, Short Stories, etc., expressing his thoughts on matters of the Heart, Spirit, Consciousness and Humanity. His primary focus is that of Love, Peace and Understanding!

Bill says . . .

I have always likened Life to that of a Garden. So, for me, Life is simply about the Seeds we Sow and Nourish. All things we "Think and Do", will "Be" Cause and eventually manifest itself to being an "Effect" within our own personal "Existences" and "Experiences" . . . whether it be Fruit, Flowers, Weeds or Barren Landscapes! Bill highly regards the Fruits of his Labor and wishes that everyone would thus go on to plant "Lovely" Seeds on "Good Ground" in their own Gardens of Life!

to connect with Bill, he is all things Inner Child

www.iaminnerchild.com

Personal Web Site

www.iamjustbill.com

William S. Peters, Sr.

Isolation ~ Empowerment ~ Confusion

There are most certainly times
When I become confused
By all the noise and clutter,
And I find embracing the need for
ISOLATION

It is only then
Do I feel empowered
Once I 're-gather myself
And refocus
On the path uncluttered

And i

I speak often
To my ancestors
And other loved ones
Whom I have lost

I too hope
That when my moment
Of reconciliation arrives
I will be able to cross
That bridge made of rainbows
And once again embrace
The objects of my
Fathomless love

I have hopes
For this life
And the next
That my soul will find balance
Between the 'in' and 'ex' trinsic expressions
Of my existence

Memories flood my reason
And in spite of myself,
The longing consumes me,
And still I will not yeild
Or fully submit

What is this tryst
I have between fiction and fact
That plays its mesmerizing music
That drunkens my resolve
And has me fractally accepting
Kaliedescopic reasoning
As a verity?

William S. Peters, Sr.

The deeper I dig
The more I realize
My shallowness
And the futility
Of my self-proclaimed
Understanding

I somehow realized
That not all open doors
Were meant to be entered
Nor exited,
Now are all windows
Meant to be opened

There is a light that
Sneaks through
The closed blinds
That affirms that
There is a Sun,
There is a Moon,
And they each have
Their purpose
.....
Me, i am upon my knees
Scratching in the dirt
In the darkness
Seeking immutable treasures
Hoping to clone my higher self
And bind it with some permanence
To my ultimate expectations
As to why I am here,
And to what end
Does this journey proceed

I honor each and every footstep
I have taken up to my 'Here',
And 'Now'
I acknowledge the
Power of Fate and Destiny
Contrived or not
And I.....

William S. Peters, Sr.

Pleading .... for Change

I often think about this world,
Our planet
And the extensive beauty
Of the landscapes,
The waters, mountains and skies
I have been blessed
To witness,
Be it being there or
Via pictures
.... I am not only enamored,
But mesmerized and overcome
With that old phrase
We armchair philosophers
Often ask ... 'what if'

What if mankind as a whole
Exhibited its beauty,
A yet unquantified embrace
Of our higher selves

What if we never polluted
The rivers, streams and oceans,
The air and the land,
Or our spirits and minds
With waste, greed and covetous things
And other proprietary exclusions
To be harbored by the few,
Excluding the many

We have so many other challenges
To be faced such as
Hunger, disease, homelessness,
And more.

The sad reality is that
There is enough prosperity
To feed all of the children
Of creation ....
Yet somehow
We are able to disable
Our empathy,
Our caring,
Our hearts.

I am pleading for change,
And we must,
Or perish

William S. Peters, Sr.

September 2025 Featured Poets

Abeera Mirza

Shaswata Gangopadhyay

Shahid Abbas Shahid

Snežana Šolkotović

Abeera Mirza

Abeera Mirza

Abeera Mirza, a wordsmith with a heart of gold, weaves emotional healing through her poetry. "Writing is the tool of emotional healing." As a daughter of the majestic Mughal empire, Abeera's literary prowess shines bright. With over 200 anthology contributions, numerous awards, and a role as jury member for Maverick Writing Community, India, her impact is undeniable. Let her words be the balm to your soul.

Email: abeera.quotes@gmail.com
Facebook|Instagram: @abeera_quotes

Abeera Mirza

Nobody Knows

Slowly crying and finding a solution on my own,
Smiling, laughing is what they see and know.

Depression is not that easy to move on,
It feels like you're in a prison shaped like a cone.

Being myself is what I'm aiming for,
The one who's being charming.

Now all I do is to cry and hide,
Need an arms who's open wide.

Telling that I'm not that fine at all,
There's no friends to be call.

The one who's willing to listen,
Who's willing to watch my glisten.

Only my pillow knows how heavy my tears are,
Only my blanket knows how painful my heart is.

Only my room knows how silent I am,
Only my wall knows how tired I am!

Alone

Sitting in the dark and quiet place,
To vanish my thoughts which I think was safe.

Delete, cancel, and erase was in my mind,
Those good memories that still now rewind.

I have to do this on my own,
In these days you've never been shown.

I'm done crying over those memories of us,
So I need to move forward and forget the past.

I know it was hard for me to do it.
But I'm so tired of that bullshit.
I am slowly liking my own existence,
Which I think leads me to a good presence.

I hope you're happy with your new lover,
That our love story went to the game over.

Don't worry I'll be okay soon,
Just like the marvelous moon.

But for now let me feel the grief of your lost.
My broken heart and those heavy tears is more than a cost.

Going to a place where nobody saw me cried,
Dealing with the pain that makes me really tired.

Abeera Mirza

A New Beginning

There are some closed doors,
They will stay close and help in opening more.

If some doors stay close,
Don't worry it means a new one is chosen.

New beginnings are about to open,
Just don't stop hoping.

Bad days will end,
Good days will begin.

If some doors are getting shut,
They strengthen our gut to wait.

Each door leads to a new path,
Each path has its own math.

Life is part of the heavyweight road,
But it will assist how to take load.

Shaswata Gangopadhyay

Shaswata Gangopadhyay

Shaswata Gangopadhyay is one of the Prominent faces of Contemporary Bengali Poetry, who started writing in Mid 90's. His poems have been published in all six continents in more than 150 International Journals and Anthologies through translations in 7-8 languages.

His book of Poems: Inhabitant of Pluto Planet, Offspring of Monster, Holes of Red Crabs, In the city of myth and mushroom, Poems of Shaswata Gangopadhyay and Rhododendron Café. He has also been invited to read his poems in UK, USA, France, Australia, South Africa, Colombia and Portugal Virtual Book Fair.

He has been invited to Paris, Vienna and Frankfurt to read his poems. This year, He was invited to Prestigious 'Gateway Lit Fest' at Mumbai to read his poems.

Leopard

In fact I'm a leopard, my craze being to hunt the prey
who is unprotected and where, I search for, whose intimacy with

such a friend,- that young boy, when standing before
looks more sexy even than God, on chin full of beards

and on that soft hairs plays quiet smooth wind,
I gave her an evil omen, the girl heard that foreboding

After that, leaving her companion, and having the smell of my body
she has come with her face down, on her chin

I unfasten my palm, not palm even, as if black hole
suddenly it'll drag one into a hollow pit, just raise your eyes to look

Yes, I'm that man, whom you on the night of fantasy
demolished in your own way with caresses and wounds

have you identified me? I'm acquainted with you since long time back
If I'm a leopard, then you're a she-leopard in reality

Gigolo

I watch him from a distance-the young guy
Standing at Free School Street with a hanky tied to his right hand

Tall in height, he appears to be a sailor unknown
Upon his deep blue T-shirt glows a shining line :
'If being sexy is a crime, arrest me soon'
The girls beside measure him with an oblique look
Some of them lick their lips, as if it's storm in the wild desert,
Where snakes crawl with hissing sounds,
Such is the blazing pain all over the pores of the body

Halogen flashing, serially on the pavements night descends
As if with endless froths from the corks of champagne,
- The 'night' which is also a woman fasting,
Beaconing the boy from inside of a black car
And then, taking him in it, starts towards no destination

An Egyptian Folk Tale

Don't throw stones at a fellow who truly loves you
those stones will come back to you someday or other

It is an Egyptian folk tale, the written version in the proverb
but you didn't obey it, rather as a first lover
you ditched him, leaving him alone
putting chewing gum casually in your mouth
at 8 o'clock past 10 in the morning,
you are crossing the quiet desert,
no mirage is visible, only broken skeletons
of camels lie scattered here and there
sometimes after the sun will look like a ruthless hammer
after pulling out from your rucksack the last bottle of soft drinks
you being exhausted, will roll on the ground senseless
sense when regained, you listen to the wind of the storm :
It's the curse of the God of sands and deserts :

Throughout your life you all alone will go on searching water
you will earn money, enjoy solvency, but never you will get a beloved

Shahid Abbas Shahid

Shahid Abbas Shahid

Shahid Abbas Shahid hailed from Kirpala Tandlianwala, Faisalabad, Pakistan, is a distinguished nature poet, versatile in English, Urdu, and Punjabi. His literary endeavors have yielded two acclaimed books: "Words from Nature" and "We Speak in Syllables."

Human Hands, Earth's Plea

Human hands, destructive might,
Ravaging Earth, day and endless night,
No immediate action, no reprieve,
Heaven turned hell, our future to retrieve.

The climate's beauty fades from sight,
Why wait for more devastation's night?
Our actions, a dismal parade,
Save our generations, now displayed.

Loyal to Mother Earth, we stand,
Value all creatures, hand in hand,
Leaders, signatures aside,
Action, not words, we must provide.

Humanity, wise up, change your ways,
Greed's heavy cost, in endless days,
Open wisdom's book, and read,
Act now, let's suffer, ages ahead.

Who am I?

Ruined yet alive,
Protected yet dead.
Uncertainty reigns,
Fear envelops my sphere.

Am I dead or alive?
Life claims me, Death denies,
I question my existence.
Who am I? Void of self,
My soul wanders, lost.

A Beauty

On her father's grave, she sits alone,
Sun setting, birds' final tone.
Eyes closed, seeking spirit's peace,
Connecting deeply, heart's release.

A heavy-lidded gaze meets mine,
Sorrow's weight, heart's decline.
"Life's empty," she whispers low,
"Everything's lost, my father is gone."

He once said, "Precious daughter, mine."
Now, in silence, she reminds me,
Visiting graves, a lonely cry,
"Still your daughter," she says, wondering why.

Snežana Šolkotović

Snežana Šolkotović

Snežana Šolkotović was born in 1962. She is a teacher of classroom elementary scool. Writing is her hobby. She has published poems and stories for children and adults in 63 different books. A number of her poems and stories are featured in numerous national and international anthologies, collections and journals, as well. She has won prestigious awards at domestic and international competitions.

Books

My life is a book
there is my childhood,
a girl who rejoices
and loves the world around her...
Between the lines
is laughter, great love,
Moments like a colorful meadow,
 wind overwhelm the soul of delight.

In them are the first love,
first knowledge of life
learned letters, numbers,
the secret of a kiss trough the fence.

Books are dreams and desires,
first experience, written song,
the book is a friend in solitude,
help in doubt when you need advice...,help.
Books are memories
In time they recount what happened
I am in them
an untold story.

Friendship Is…

Friendship is a bridge
which connects the two banks of the river,
two souls with love,
hand in hand…
Friendship is words
with whom happiness and sorrow are shared,
when it's hardest for you in solitude
and you have the support of your friend...
Friendship is like the scent of a flower
which brightens your day,
shared secret,
peaceful dream...
Friendship is a bridge
between two similar souls,
sometimes he is a guest in our hearts,
the sound of a song that breaks nostalgia.

There...

I was born there,
I took the first step there, I said the first word
There is my homeland, my love,
There I opened the door of the soul...
There are my sunny dawns,
childhood dreams, my family,
a lump of earth, old house,
lantern light confusing fireflies.
There the sky is especially blue,
the Danube River boasts waves,
there are huge fields, flower meadows,
the song of life is created with delight ...
I carry the scent of linden in my soul
Stories of the past remind me of who I am,
sheaves of wheat keep my secrets
this is my homeland,
I know very well what a breath of freedom means...
Peace and friendship, messages of love are sent around the world
That's what binds people together,
This is my homeland, Serbia,
Homeland except this, I have no other...

Remembering

our fallen soldiers of verse

Janet Perkins Caldwell
February 14, 1959 ~ September 20, 2016

Alan W. Jankowski
16 March 1961 ~ 10 March 2017

Shareef Abdur Rasheed
30 May 1945 ~ 11 February 2025

The Butterfly Effect

"IS" in effect

Inner Child Press News

Published Books by Poetry Posse Members

We are so excited to share and announce a few of the current books, as well as the new and upcoming books of some of our Poetry Posse authors.

Inner Child Press News

On the following pages we present to you ...

Alicja Maria Kuberska

Jackie Davis Allen

Gail Weston Shazor

hülya n. yılmaz

Nizar Sartawi

Elizabeth E. Castillo

Faleeha Hassan

Fahredin Shehu

Kimberly Burnham

Caroline 'Ceri' Nazareno

Eliza Segiet

Teresa E. Gallion

Mutawaf Shaheed

William S. Peters, Sr.

Now Available
www.innerchildpress.com

KREW ŻYCIA
The Blood of Life

Eliza Segiet

Translated by Dorota Stępińska

Now Available
www.innerchildpress.com

Inner Child Press News

Now Available

Inner Child Press News

www.innerchildpress.com

Now Available

www.innerchildpress.com

Inner Child Press News
Now Available
www.innerchildpress.com

Now Available
www.innerchildpress.com

Inner Child Press News

Now Available
www.innerchildpress.com

Now Available
www.innerchildpress.com

Inner Child Press News

Now Available
www.innerchildpress.com

Now Available
www.innerchildpress.com

Inner Child Press News

Now Available
www.innerchildpress.com

Now Available
www.innerchildpress.com

Inner Child Press News

Now Available
www.innerchildpress.com

Now Available at
www.innerchildpress.com

Inner Child Press News

Now Available at
www.amazon.com/gp/product/B08MYL5B7S/ref=dbs_a_def_rwt_hsch_vapi_tkin_p1_i2

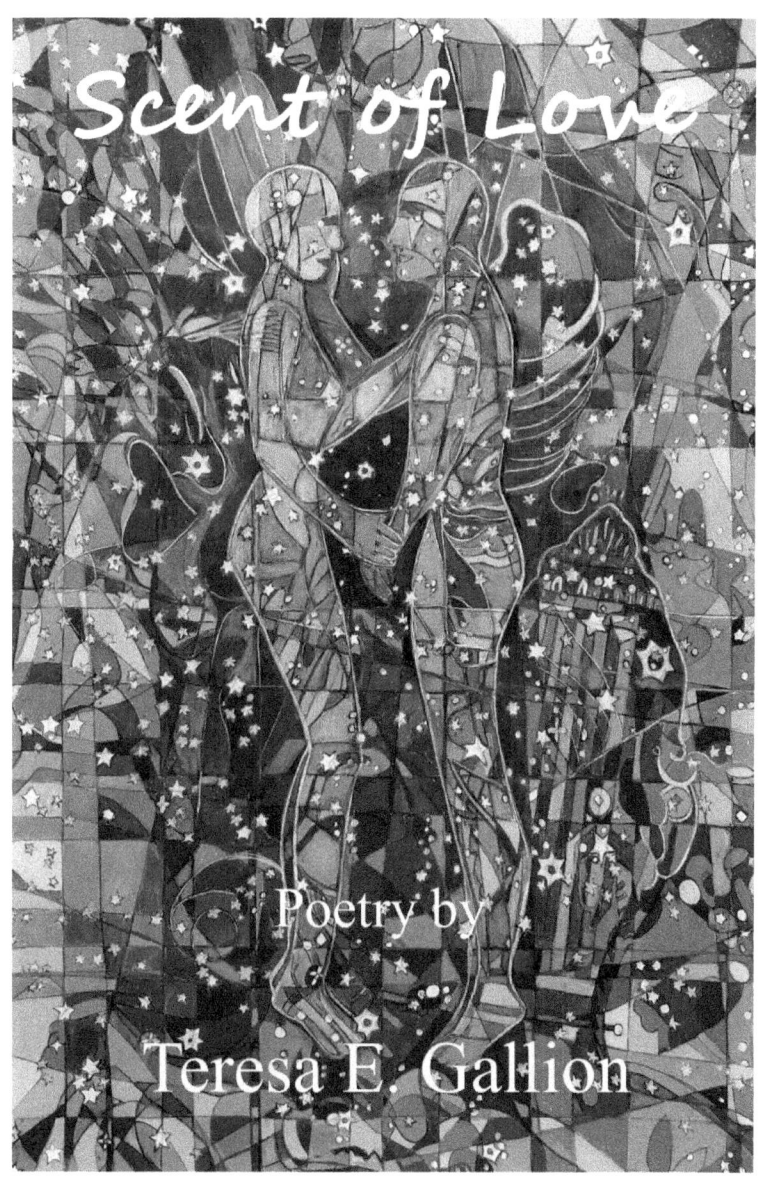

Now Available
www.innerchildpress.com

Inner Child Press News

Now Available
www.innerchildpress.com

Now Available
www.innerchildpress.com

Inner Child Press News

Now Available
www.innerchildpress.com

Now Available
www.innerchildpress.com

Inner Child Press News

Now Available
www.innerchildpress.com

Now Available
www.innerchildpress.com

Now Available
www.innerchildpress.com

Inner Child Press News

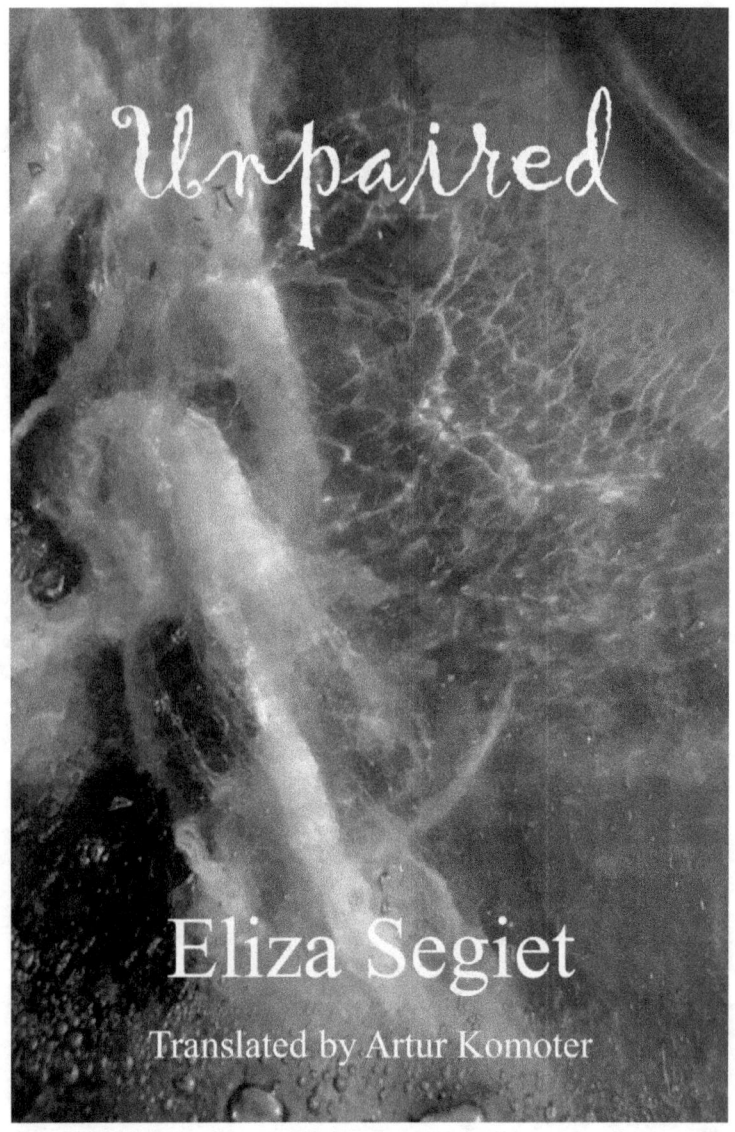

Now Available
www.innerchildpress.com

Private Issue
www.innerchildpress.com

Inner Child Press News

Now Available at
www.innerchildpress.com

Now Available at
www.innerchildpress.com

Inner Child Press News

Now Available at
www.innerchildpress.com

Now Available at
www.innerchildpress.com

Inner Child Press News

HERENOW

FAHREDIN SHEHU

Now Available at
www.innerchildpress.com

Now Available at
www.innerchildpress.com

Inner Child Press News

Dark Side of the Moon

Jackie Davis Allen

Now Available at
www.innerchildpress.com

Now Available at
www.innerchildpress.com

Now Available at
www.innerchildpress.com

Now Available at
www.innerchildpress.com

Inner Child Press News

Now Available at
www.innerchildpress.com

Now Available at
www.innerchildpress.com

Inner Child Press News

Now Available at
www.innerchildpress.com

Now Available at
www.innerchildpress.com

Now Available
www.innerchildpress.com

Inner Child Press News

Other Anthological works from

Inner Child Press International

www.innerchildpress.com

Inner Child Press Anthologies

Shareef
a soldier for
Allah

Patriarch, Activist & Humanitarian

Friends of the Pen

Now Available
www.innerchildpress.com/anthologies

Inner Child Press Anthologies

Now Available
www.innerchildpress.com

Inner Child Press Anthologies

I want my poetry to... *volume* 4

the conscious poets

inspired by . . . Monte Smith

Now Available
www.innerchildpress.com/anthologies

Now Available
www.innerchildpress.com/anthologies

Inner Child Press Anthologies

Now Available
www.worldhealingworldpeacepoetry.com

Inner Child Press Anthologies

Now Available
www.innerchildpress.com/anthologies

Inner Child Press Anthologies

Now Available
www.worldhealingworldpeacepoetry.com

Inner Child Press Anthologies

Now Available
www.innerchildpress.com/anthologies

Inner Child Press Anthologies

Inner Child Press International
&
The Year of the Poet
present

Poetry

the best of 2020

Poets of the World

Now Available
www.innerchildpress.com/anthologies

Inner Child Press Anthologies

Now Available
www.innerchildpress.com/anthologies

Inner Child Press Anthologies

Now Available
www.innerchildpress.com/anthologies

Inner Child Press Anthologies

Now Available
www.innerchildpress.com/anthologies

Inner Child Press Anthologies

Now Available
www.innerchildpress.com/anthologies

Inner Child Press Anthologies

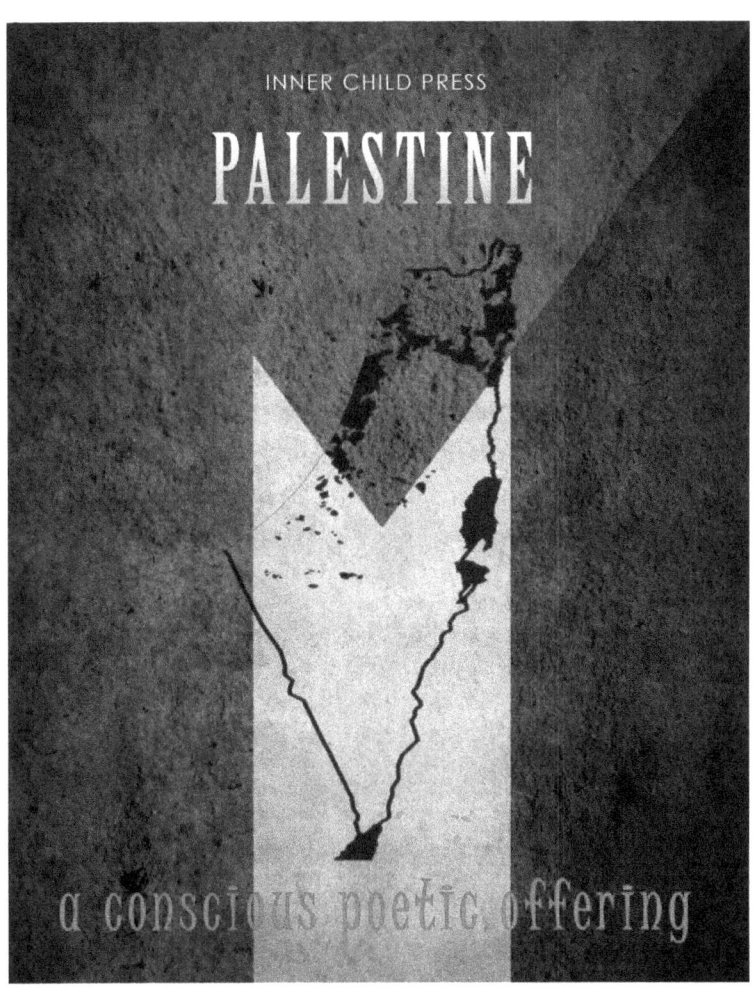

Now Available
www.innerchildpress.com/anthologies

Inner Child Press Anthologies

Now Available
www.innerchildpress.com/anthologies

Inner Child Press Anthologies

Now Available
www.innerchildpress.com/anthologies

Inner Child Press Anthologies

Now Available
www.worldhealingworldpeacepoetry.com

Inner Child Press Anthologies

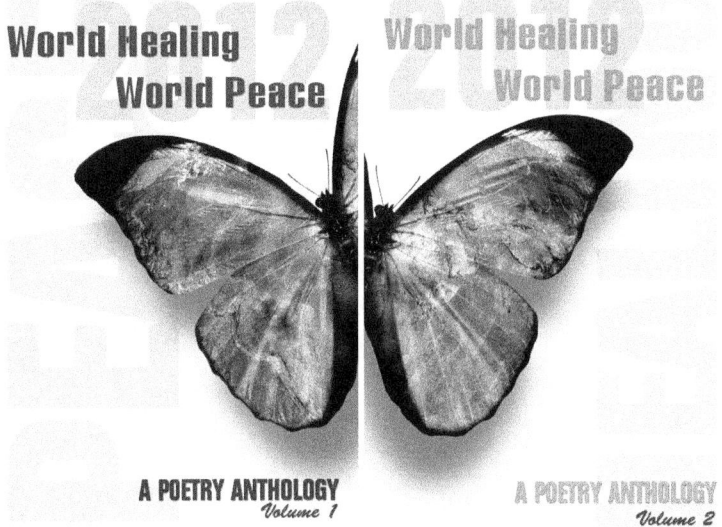

Now Available
www.worldhealingworldpeacepoetry.com

Inner Child Press Anthologies

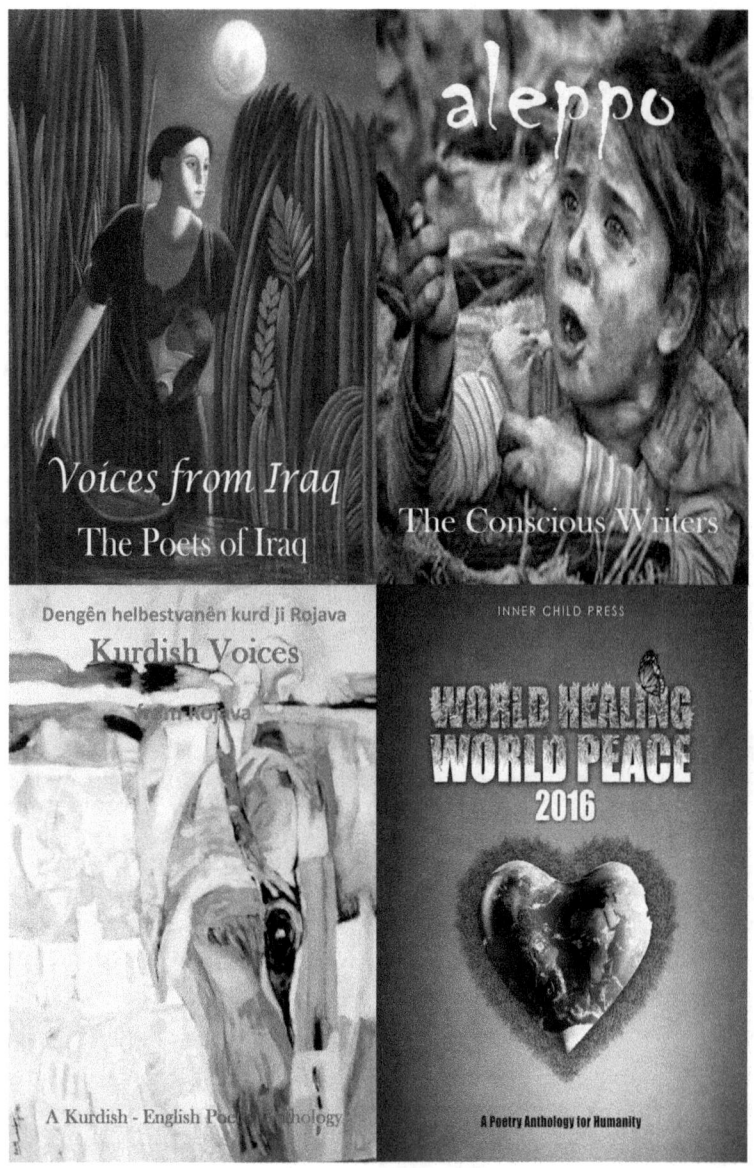

Now Available
www.innerchildpress.com/anthologies

Inner Child Press Anthologies

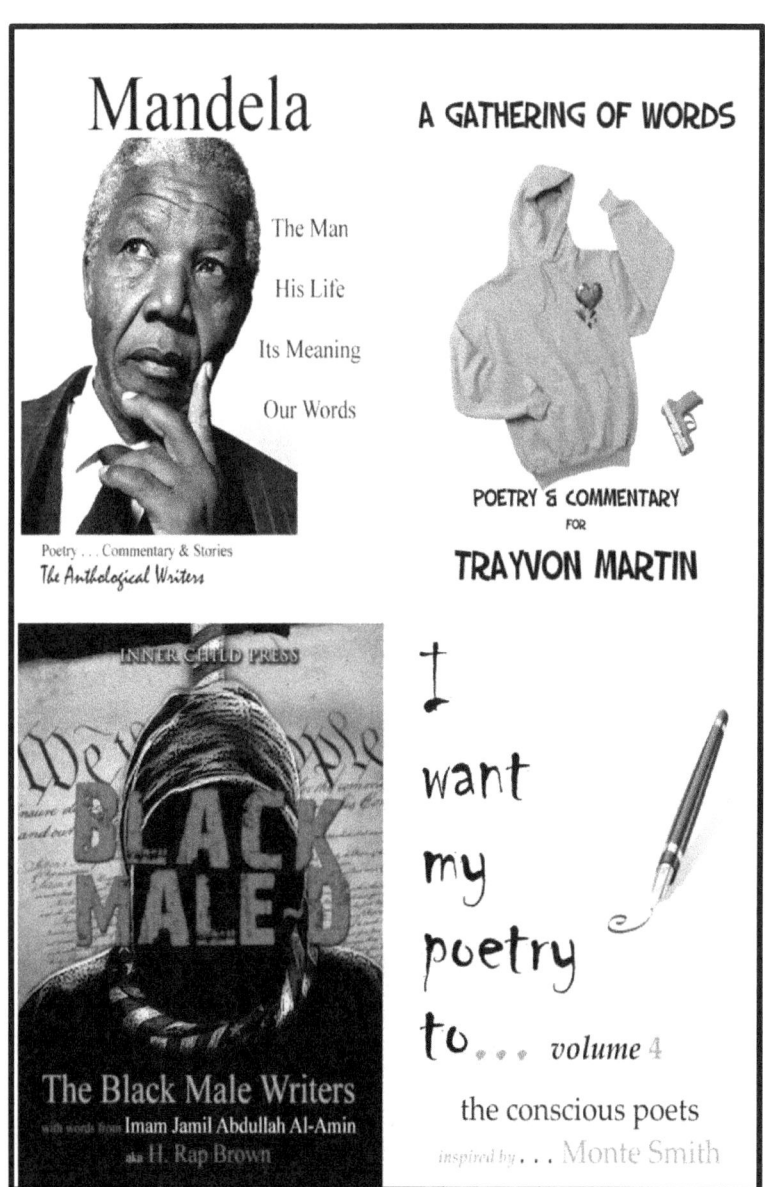

Now Available
www.innerchildpress.com/anthologies

Inner Child Press Anthologies

Now Available
www.innerchildpress.com/anthologies

Inner Child Press Anthologies

Now Available
www.innerchildpress.com/anthologies

Inner Child Press Anthologies

Now Available
www.innerchildpress.com/anthologies

Now Available
www.innerchildpress.com/the-year-of-the-poet

Inner Child Press Anthologies

Now Available
www.innerchildpress.com/the-year-of-the-poet

Inner Child Press Anthologies

Now Available
www.innerchildpress.com/the-year-of-the-poet

Inner Child Press Anthologies

Now Available
www.innerchildpress.com/the-year-of-the-poet

Inner Child Press Anthologies

The Year of the Poet II
May 2015

May's Featured Poets
Geri Algeri
Akin Mosi Chinnery
Anna Jakubczak

Emeralds

The Poetry Posse 2015
Jamie Bond * Gail Weston Shazor * Albert 'Infinite' Carrasco
Siddartha Beth Pierce * Janet P. Caldwell * Tony Henninger
Joe DaVerbal Minddancer * Neetu Wali * Shareef Abdur – Rasheed
Kimberly Burnham * Ann White * Keith Alan Hamilton
Katherine Wyatt * Fahredin Shehu * Hülya N. Yılmaz
Teresa E. Gallion * Jackie Allen * William S. Peters. Sr.

The Year of the Poet II
June 2015

June's Featured Poets
Anahit Arustamyan * Ivette D. Mussell * Regina A. Walker

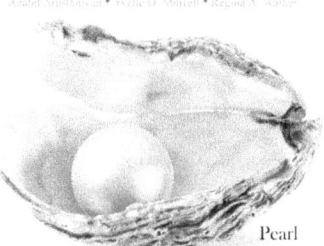

Pearl

The Poetry Posse 2015
Jamie Bond * Gail Weston Shazor * Albert 'Infinite' Carrasco
Siddartha Beth Pierce * Janet P. Caldwell * Tony Henninger
Joe DaVerbal Minddancer * Neetu Wali * Shareef Abdur – Rasheed
Kimberly Burnham * Ann White * Keith Alan Hamilton
Katherine Wyatt * Fahredin Shehu * Hülya N. Yılmaz
Teresa E. Gallion * Jackie Allen * William S. Peters. Sr.

The Year of the Poet II
July 2015

The Featured Poets for July, 2015
Abhik Shome * Christina Neal * Robert Neal

Rubies

The Poetry Posse 2015
Jamie Bond * Gail Weston Shazor * Albert 'Infinite' Carrasco
Siddartha Beth Pierce * Janet P. Caldwell * Tony Henninger
Joe DaVerbal Minddancer * Neetu Wali * Shareef Abdur – Rasheed
Kimberly Burnham * Ann White * Keith Alan Hamilton
Katherine Wyatt * Fahredin Shehu * Hülya N. Yılmaz
Teresa E. Gallion * Jackie Allen * William S. Peters. Sr.

The Year of the Poet II
August 2015

Peridot

Featured Poets
Gayle Howell
Ann Chalasz
Christopher Schultz

The Poetry Posse 2015
Jamie Bond * Gail Weston Shazor * Albert 'Infinite' Carrasco
Siddartha Beth Pierce * Janet P. Caldwell * Tony Henninger
Joe DaVerbal Minddancer * Neetu Wali * Shareef Abdur – Rasheed
Kimberly Burnham * Ann White * Keith Alan Hamilton
Katherine Wyatt * Fahredin Shehu * Hülya N. Yılmaz
Teresa E. Gallion * Jackie Allen * William S. Peters. Sr.

Now Available
www.innerchildpress.com/the-year-of-the-poet

Inner Child Press Anthologies

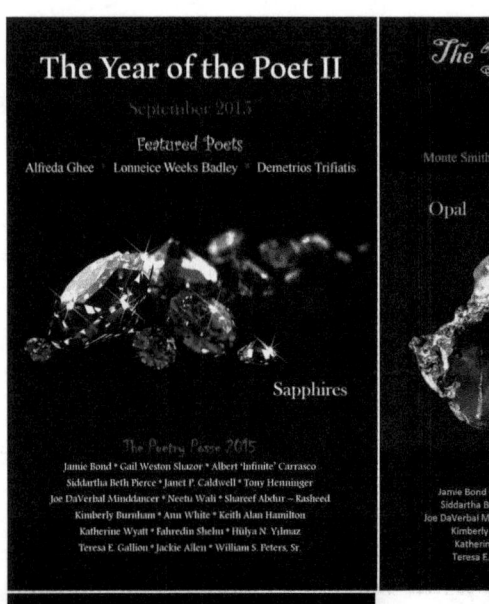

Now Available
www.innerchildpress.com/the-year-of-the-poet

Now Available
www.innerchildpress.com/the-year-of-the-poet

Inner Child Press Anthologies

Now Available
www.innerchildpress.com/the-year-of-the-poet

Inner Child Press Anthologies

Now Available
www.innerchildpress.com/the-year-of-the-poet

Inner Child Press Anthologies

Now Available
www.innerchildpress.com/the-year-of-the-poet

Inner Child Press Anthologies

Now Available
www.innerchildpress.com/the-year-of-the-poet

Inner Child Press Anthologies

The Year of the Poet IV
September 2017

Featured Poets
Martina Reisz Newberry
Ameer Nassir
Christine Fulco Neal
Robert Neal

The Elm Tree

The Poetry Posse 2017

Gail Weston Shazor * Caroline Nazareno * Bismay Mohanty
Teresa E. Gallion * Anna Jakubczak Vel Ratty Adalan
Joe DaVerbal Minddancer * Shareef Abdur – Rasheed
Albert Carrasco * Kimberly Burnham * Elizabeth Castillo
Hülya N. Yılmaz * Faleeha Hassan * Jackie Davis Allen
Jen Walls * Nizar Sartawi * * William S. Peters, Sr.

The Year of the Poet IV
October 2017

Featured Poets
Ahmed Abu Saleem
Nedal Al-Qaeim
Sadeddin Shahin

The Black Walnut Tree

The Poetry Posse 2017

Gail Weston Shazor * Caroline Nazareno * Bismay Mohanty
Teresa E. Gallion * Anna Jakubczak Vel Ratty Adalan
Joe DaVerbal Minddancer * Shareef Abdur – Rasheed
Albert Carrasco * Kimberly Burnham * Elizabeth Castillo
Hülya N. Yılmaz * Faleeha Hassan * Jackie Davis Allen
Jen Walls * Nizar Sartawi * * William S. Peters, Sr.

The Year of the Poet IV
November 2017

Featured Poets
Kay Peters
Alfreda D. Ghee
Gabriella Garofalo
Rosemary Cappello

The Tree of Life

The Poetry Posse 2017

Gail Weston Shazor * Caroline Nazareno * Bismay Mohanty
Teresa E. Gallion * Anna Jakubczak Vel Ratty Adalan
Joe DaVerbal Minddancer * Shareef Abdur – Rasheed
Albert Carrasco * Kimberly Burnham * Elizabeth Castillo
Hülya N. Yılmaz * Faleeha Hassan * Jackie Davis Allen
Jen Walls * Nizar Sartawi * William S. Peters, Sr.

The Year of the Poet IV
December 2017

Featured Poets
Justice Clarke
Mariel M. Pabroa
Kiley Brown

The Fig Tree

The Poetry Posse 2017

Gail Weston Shazor * Caroline Nazareno * Bismay Mohanty
Teresa E. Gallion * Anna Jakubczak Vel Ratty Adalan
Joe DaVerbal Minddancer * Shareef Abdur – Rasheed
Albert Carrasco * Kimberly Burnham * Elizabeth Castillo
Hülya N. Yılmaz * Faleeha Hassan * Jackie Davis Allen
Jen Walls * Nizar Sartawi * William S. Peters, Sr.

Now Available

www.innerchildpress.com/the-year-of-the-poet

Inner Child Press Anthologies

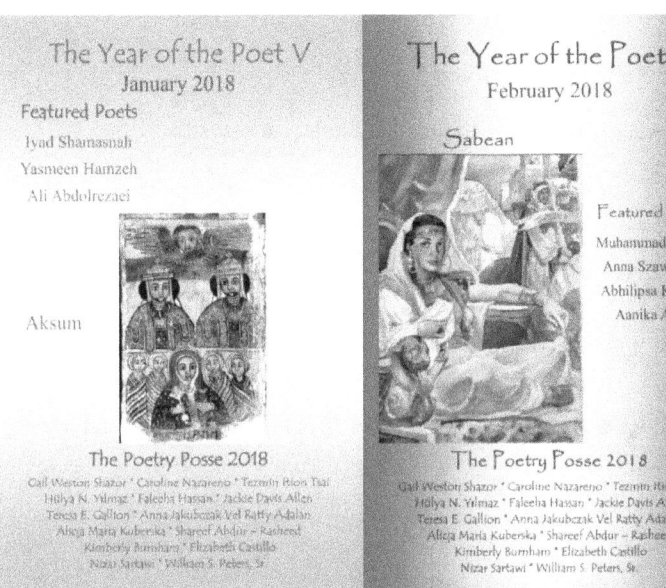

Now Available
www.innerchildpress.com/the-year-of-the-poet

Inner Child Press Anthologies

Now Available
www.innerchildpress.com/the-year-of-the-poet

Now Available
www.innerchildpress.com/the-year-of-the-poet

Inner Child Press Anthologies

The Year of the Poet VI
January 2019

Indigenous North Americans

Featured Poets

Houda Elfchtali
Anthony Briscoe
Iram Fatima 'Ashi'
Dr. K. K. Mathew

Dream Catcher

The Poetry Posse 2019

Gail Weston Shazor * Joe Paire * Hülya N. Yılmaz
Jackie Davis Allen * Caroline 'Cev' Nazareno
Alicja Maria Kuberska * Teresa E. Gallion
Kimberly Burnham * Shareef Abdur – Rasheed
Ashok K. Bhargava * Elizabeth Castillo * Swapna Behera
Tezmin Ition Tsai * William S. Peters, Sr.

The Year of the Poet VI
February 2019

Featured Poets
Marek Łukaszewicz * Bharati Nayak
Aida G. Roque * Jean-Jacques Fournier

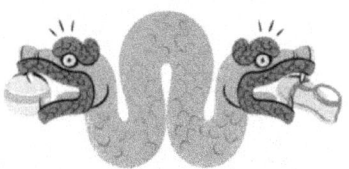

Meso-America

The Poetry Posse 2019

Gail Weston Shazor * Albert Carrasco * Hülya N. Yılmaz
Jackie Davis Allen * Caroline Nazareno * Eliza Segiet
Alicja Maria Kuberska * Teresa E. Gallion * Joe Paire
Kimberly Burnham * Shareef Abdur – Rasheed
Ashok K. Bhargava * Elizabeth Castillo * Swapna Behera
Tezmin Ition Tsai * William S. Peters, Sr.

The Year of the Poet VI
March 2019

Featured Poets
Enesa Mahmić * Sylwia K. Malinowska
Shurook Hammond * Anwer Ghani

The Caribbean

The Poetry Posse 2019

Gail Weston Shazor * Albert Carrasco * Hülya N. Yılmaz
Jackie Davis Allen * Caroline Nazareno * Eliza Segiet
Alicja Maria Kuberska * Teresa E. Gallion * Joe Paire
Kimberly Burnham * Shareef Abdur – Rasheed
Ashok K. Bhargava * Elizabeth Castillo * Swapna Behera
Tezmin Ition Tsai * William S. Peters, Sr.

The Year of the Poet VI
April 2019

Featured Poets
DL Davis * Michelle Joan Barulich
Lulëzim Haziri * Faleeha Hassan

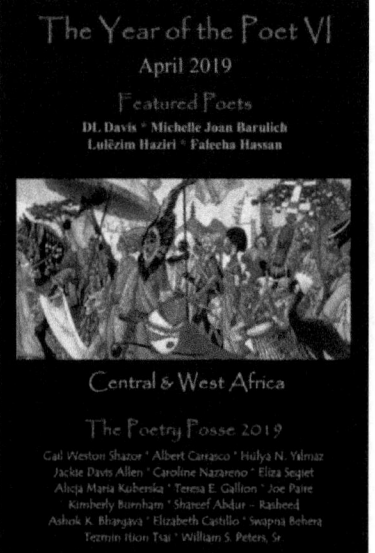

Central & West Africa

The Poetry Posse 2019

Gail Weston Shazor * Albert Carrasco * Hülya N. Yılmaz
Jackie Davis Allen * Caroline Nazareno * Eliza Segiet
Alicja Maria Kuberska * Teresa E. Gallion * Joe Paire
Kimberly Burnham * Shareef Abdur – Rasheed
Ashok K. Bhargava * Elizabeth Castillo * Swapna Behera
Tezmin Ition Tsai * William S. Peters, Sr.

Now Available
www.innerchildpress.com/the-year-of-the-poet

Now Available
www.innerchildpress.com/the-year-of-the-poet

Inner Child Press Anthologies

Now Available
www.innerchildpress.com/the-year-of-the-poet

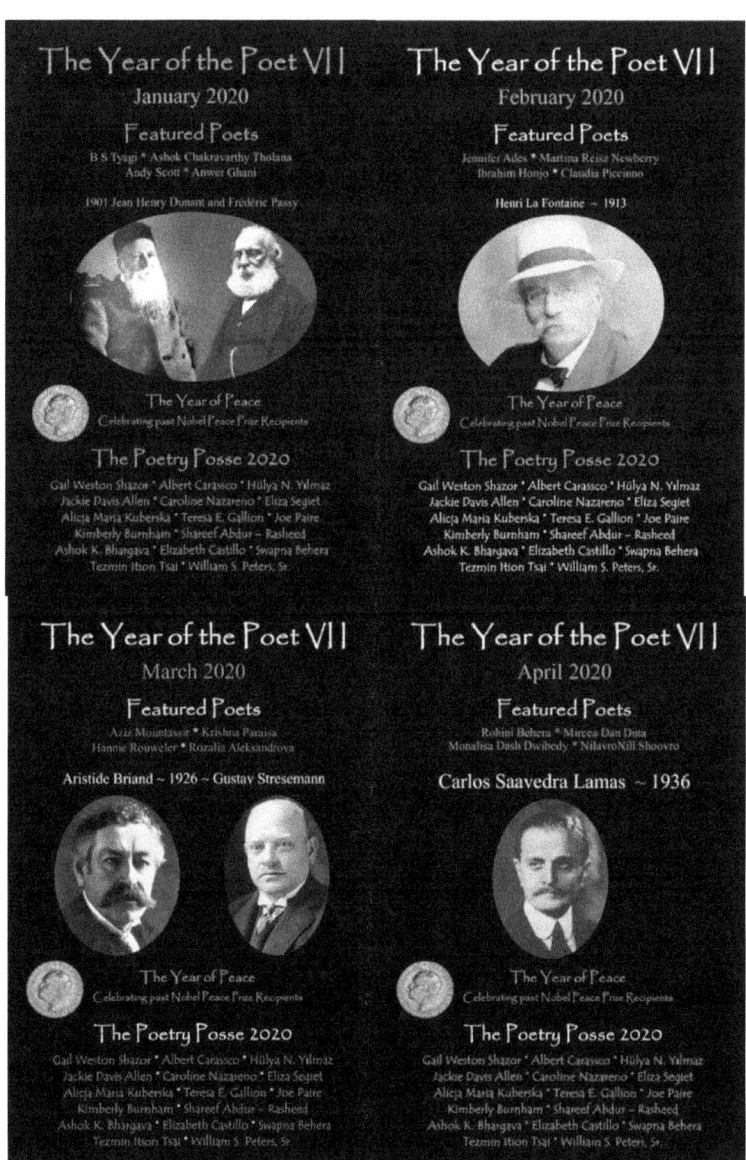

Now Available
www.innerchildpress.com/the-year-of-the-poet

Inner Child Press Anthologies

The Year of the Poet VII
May 2020

Featured Poets
Alok Kumar Ray * Eden S. Trinidad
Franco Barbato * Izabela Zubko

Ralph Bunche ~ 1950

The Year of Peace
Celebrating past Nobel Peace Prize Recipients

The Poetry Posse 2020

Gail Weston Shazor * Albert Carasco * Hülya N. Yılmaz
Jackie Davis Allen * Caroline Nazareno * Eliza Segiet
Alicja Maria Kuberska * Teresa E. Gallion * Joe Paire
Kimberly Burnham * Shareef Abdur - Rasheed
Ashok K. Bhargava * Elizabeth Castillo * Swapna Behera
Tezmin Ition Tsai * William S. Peters, Sr.

The Year of the Poet VII
June 2020

Featured Poets
Eftichia Kapardeli * Metin Cengiz
Hussein Habasch * Kosh K Mathew

Albert John Lutuli ~ 1960

The Year of Peace
Celebrating past Nobel Peace Prize Recipients

The Poetry Posse 2020

Gail Weston Shazor * Albert Carasco * Hülya N. Yılmaz
Jackie Davis Allen * Caroline Nazareno * Eliza Segiet
Alicja Maria Kuberska * Teresa E. Gallion * Joe Paire
Kimberly Burnham * Shareef Abdur - Rasheed
Ashok K. Bhargava * Elizabeth Castillo * Swapna Behera
Tezmin Ition Tsai * William S. Peters, Sr.

The Year of the Poet VII
July 2020

Featured Poets
Mykola Martyniuk * Orbindu Ganga
Roula Pollard * Karn Praktisha

Norman Ernest Borlaug ~ 1970

The Year of Peace
Celebrating past Nobel Peace Prize Recipients

The Poetry Posse 2020

Gail Weston Shazor * Albert Carasco * Hülya N. Yılmaz
Jackie Davis Allen * Caroline Nazareno * Eliza Segiet
Alicja Maria Kuberska * Teresa E. Gallion * Joe Paire
Kimberly Burnham * Shareef Abdur - Rasheed
Ashok K. Bhargava * Elizabeth Castillo * Swapna Behera
Tezmin Ition Tsai * William S. Peters, Sr.

The Year of the Poet VII
August 2020

Featured Poets
Dr Pragya Suman * Chinh Nguyen
Srinivas Vasudev * Ugwu Leonard Ifeanyi, Jr.

Adolfo Pérez Esquivel ~ 1980

The Year of Peace
Celebrating past Nobel Peace Prize Recipients

The Poetry Posse 2020

Gail Weston Shazor * Albert Carasco * Hülya N. Yılmaz
Jackie Davis Allen * Caroline Nazareno * Eliza Segiet
Alicja Maria Kuberska * Teresa E. Gallion * Joe Paire
Kimberly Burnham * Shareef Abdur - Rasheed
Ashok K. Bhargava * Elizabeth Castillo * Swapna Behera
Tezmin Ition Tsai * William S. Peters, Sr.

Now Available
www.innerchildpress.com/the-year-of-the-poet

Inner Child Press Anthologies

The Year of the Poet VIII
January 2021

Featured Global Poets
Andrew Scott * Debaprasanna Biswas
Shakil Kalam * Changming Yuan

Banksy's The Girl with the Pierced Eardrum

Poetry ... Ekphrasticly Speaking
The Poetry Posse 2020
Gail Weston Shazor * Albert Carasso * Hülya N. Yilmaz
Jackie Davis Allen * Caroline Nazareno * Eliza Segiet
Alicja Maria Kuberska * Teresa E. Gallion * Joe Paire
Kimberly Burnham * Shareef Abdur - Rasheed
Ashok K. Bhargava * Elizabeth Castillo * Swapna Behera
Tezmin Ition Tsai * William S. Peters, Sr.

The Year of the Poet VIII
February 2021

Featured Global Poets
T. Ramesh Babu * Ruchida Barman
Neptune Barman * Faleeha Hassan

Emory Douglas : 1968 Olympics mural

Poetry ... Ekphrasticly Speaking
The Poetry Posse 2021
Gail Weston Shazor * Albert Carasso * Hülya N. Yilmaz
Jackie Davis Allen * Caroline Nazareno * Eliza Segiet
Alicja Maria Kuberska * Teresa E. Gallion * Joe Paire
Kimberly Burnham * Shareef Abdur - Rasheed
Ashok K. Bhargava * Elizabeth Castillo * Swapna Behera
Tezmin Ition Tsai * William S. Peters, Sr.

The Year of the Poet VIII
March 2021

Featured Global Poets
Claudia Piccinno * Mohammed Jabr
Luzviminda Rivera * Nigar Arif

Tatyana Fazlalizadeh

Poetry ... Ekphrasticly Speaking
The Poetry Posse 2021
Gail Weston Shazor * Albert Carasso * Hülya N. Yilmaz
Jackie Davis Allen * Caroline Nazareno * Eliza Segiet
Alicja Maria Kuberska * Teresa E. Gallion * Joe Paire
Kimberly Burnham * Shareef Abdur - Rasheed
Ashok K. Bhargava * Elizabeth Castillo * Swapna Behera
Tezmin Ition Tsai * William S. Peters, Sr.

The Year of the Poet VIII
April 2021

Featured Global Poets
Katarzyna Brus- Sawczuk * Anwesha Paul
Rozalia Aleksandrova * Shahid Abbas

Pablo O'Higgins

Poetry ... Ekphrasticly Speaking
The Poetry Posse 2021
Gail Weston Shazor * Albert Carasso * Hülya N. Yilmaz
Jackie Davis Allen * Caroline Nazareno * Eliza Segiet
Alicja Maria Kuberska * Teresa E. Gallion * Joe Paire
Kimberly Burnham * Shareef Abdur - Rasheed
Ashok K. Bhargava * Elizabeth Castillo * Swapna Behera
Tezmin Ition Tsai * William S. Peters, Sr.

Now Available
www.innerchildpress.com/the-year-of-the-poet

Now Available
www.innerchildpress.com/the-year-of-the-poet

Inner Child Press Anthologies

The Year of the Poet VIII
September 2021

Featured Global Poets

Monsif Beroual * Sandesh Ghimire
Sharmila Poudel * Pavol Janik

Heather Jansch

Poetry ... Ekphrasticly Speaking

The Poetry Posse 2021

Gail Weston Shazor * Albert Carasco * Hülya N. Yılmaz
Jackie Davis Allen * Caroline Nazareno * Eliza Segiet
Alicja Maria Kuberska * Teresa E. Gallion * Joe Paire
Kimberly Burnham * Shareef Abdur – Rasheed
Ashok K. Bhargava * Elizabeth Castillo * Swapna Behera
Tezmin Ition Tsai * William S. Peters, Sr.

The Year of the Poet VIII
October 2021

Featured Global Poets

C. E. Shy * Saswata Ganguly
Suranjit Gain * Hasiba Hilal

Dale Lamphere

Poetry ... Ekphrasticly Speaking

The Poetry Posse 2021

Gail Weston Shazor * Albert Carasco * Hülya N. Yılmaz
Jackie Davis Allen * Caroline Nazareno * Eliza Segiet
Alicja Maria Kuberska * Teresa E. Gallion * Joe Paire
Kimberly Burnham * Shareef Abdur – Rasheed
Ashok K. Bhargava * Elizabeth Castillo * Swapna Behera
Tezmin Ition Tsai * William S. Peters, Sr.

The Year of the Poet VIII
November 2021

Featured Global Poets

Errol D. Bean * Ibrahim Honjo
Tanja Ajtic * Rajashree Mohapatra

Andy Goldsworthy

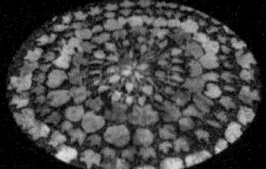

Poetry ... Ekphrasticly Speaking

The Poetry Posse 2021

Gail Weston Shazor * Albert Carasco * Hülya N. Yılmaz
Jackie Davis Allen * Caroline Nazareno * Eliza Segiet
Alicja Maria Kuberska * Teresa E. Gallion * Joe Paire
Kimberly Burnham * Shareef Abdur – Rasheed
Ashok K. Bhargava * Elizabeth Castillo * Swapna Behera
Tezmin Ition Tsai * William S. Peters, Sr.

The Year of the Poet VIII
December 2021

Featured Global Poets

Orbinda Ganga * Fadairo Tesleem
Anthony Arnold * Iyad Shamasnah

Fredric Edwin Church

Poetry ... Ekphrasticly Speaking

The Poetry Posse 2021

Gail Weston Shazor * Albert Carasco * Hülya N. Yılmaz
Jackie Davis Allen * Caroline Nazareno * Eliza Segiet
Alicja Maria Kuberska * Teresa E. Gallion * Joe Paire
Kimberly Burnham * Shareef Abdur – Rasheed
Ashok K. Bhargava * Elizabeth Castillo * Swapna Behera
Tezmin Ition Tsai * William S. Peters, Sr.

Now Available
www.innerchildpress.com/the-year-of-the-poet

Inner Child Press Anthologies

The Year of the Poet IX
January 2022

Featured Global Poets

Ratan Ghosh * Christine Neil-Wright
Andrew Scott * Ashok Kumar

Climate Change : The Ice Cap

Poetry . . . Ekphrasticly Speaking

The Poetry Posse 2021

Gail Weston Shazor * Albert Carasco * Hülya N. Yılmaz
Jackie Davis Allen * Caroline Nazareno * Eliza Segiet
Alicja Maria Kuberska * Teresa E. Gallion * Joe Paire
Kimberly Burnham * Shareef Abdur – Rasheed
Ashok K. Bhargava * Elizabeth Castillo * Swapna Behera
Tezmin Ition Tsai * William S. Peters, Sr.

The Year of the Poet IX
February 2022

Featured Global Poets

Roza Boyanova * Ramón de Jesús Núñez Duval
Mammad Ismayil * Tarana Turan Rahimli

Climate Change and Mountains

Poetry . . . Ekphrasticly Speaking

The Poetry Posse 2021

Gail Weston Shazor * Albert Carasco * Hülya N. Yılmaz
Jackie Davis Allen * Caroline Nazareno * Eliza Segiet
Alicja Maria Kuberska * Teresa E. Gallion * Joe Paire
Kimberly Burnham * Shareef Abdur – Rasheed
Ashok K. Bhargava * Elizabeth Castillo * Swapna Behera
Tezmin Ition Tsai * William S. Peters, Sr.

The Year of the Poet IX
March 2022

Featured Global Poets

Dimitris P. Kraniotis * Marlene Pasini
Kennedy Ochieng * Swayam Prashant

Climate Change and Space Debris

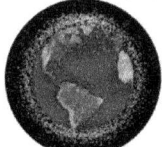

Poetry . . . Ekphrasticly Speaking

The Poetry Posse 2021

Gail Weston Shazor * Albert Carasco * Hülya N. Yılmaz
Jackie Davis Allen * Caroline Nazareno * Eliza Segiet
Alicja Maria Kuberska * Teresa E. Gallion * Joe Paire
Kimberly Burnham * Shareef Abdur – Rasheed
Ashok K. Bhargava * Elizabeth Castillo * Swapna Behera
Tezmin Ition Tsai * William S. Peters, Sr.

The Year of the Poet IX
April 2022

Featured Global Poets

Alonzo Gross * Dr. Debaprasanna Biswas
Monsif Beroual * Carol Aronoff

Climate Change and Oceans

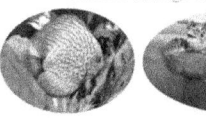

*Celebrating our 100th Edition *

Poetry . . . Ekphrasticly Speaking

The Poetry Posse 2021

Gail Weston Shazor * Albert Carasco * Hülya N. Yılmaz
Jackie Davis Allen * Caroline Nazareno * Eliza Segiet
Alicja Maria Kuberska * Teresa E. Gallion * Joe Paire
Kimberly Burnham * Shareef Abdur – Rasheed
Ashok K. Bhargava * Elizabeth Castillo * Swapna Behera
Tezmin Ition Tsai * William S. Peters, Sr.

Now Available

www.innerchildpress.com/the-year-of-the-poet

Inner Child Press Anthologies

The Year of the Poet IX
May 2022

Featured Global Poets
Ndaba Sibanda * Smrutiranjan Mohanty
Ajanta Paul * Monalisa Dash Dwibedy

Climate Change and Birds

Poetry ... Ekphrasticly Speaking

The Poetry Posse 2021
Gail Weston Shazor * Albert Carasco * Hülya N. Yılmaz
Jackie Davis Allen * Caroline Nazareno * Eliza Segiet
Alicja Maria Kuberska * Teresa E. Gallion * Joe Paire
Kimberly Burnham * Shareef Abdur – Rasheed
Ashok K. Bhargava * Elizabeth Castillo * Swapna Behera
Tezmin Ition Tsai * William S. Peters, Sr.

The Year of the Poet IX
June 2022

Featured Global Poets
Yuan Changming * Azeezat Okunlola
Tanja Ajtić * Philip Chijioke Abonyi

Climate Change and Trees

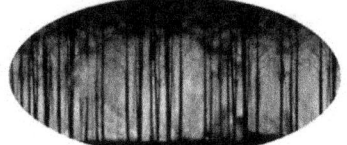

Poetry ... Ekphrasticly Speaking

The Poetry Posse 2022
Gail Weston Shazor * Albert Carasco * Hülya N. Yılmaz
Jackie Davis Allen * Caroline Nazareno * Eliza Segiet
Alicja Maria Kuberska * Teresa E. Gallion * Joe Paire
Kimberly Burnham * Shareef Abdur – Rasheed
Ashok K. Bhargava * Elizabeth Castillo * Swapna Behera
Tezmin Ition Tsai * William S. Peters, Sr.

The Year of the Poet IX
July 2022

Featured Global Poets
Michelle Joan Barulich * Mili Das
Anna Ferriero * Ujjal Mandal

Climate Change and Animals

Poetry ... Ekphrasticly Speaking

The Poetry Posse 2022
Gail Weston Shazor * Albert Carasco * Hülya N. Yılmaz
Jackie Davis Allen * Caroline Nazareno * Eliza Segiet
Alicja Maria Kuberska * Teresa E. Gallion * Joe Paire
Kimberly Burnham * Shareef Abdur – Rasheed
Ashok K. Bhargava * Elizabeth Castillo * Swapna Behera
Tezmin Ition Tsai * William S. Peters, Sr.

The Year of the Poet IX
August 2022

Featured Global Poets
Pankhuri Sinha * Abdulloh Abdumominov
Caroline Turunç * Tali Cohen Shabtai

Climate Change and Agriculture

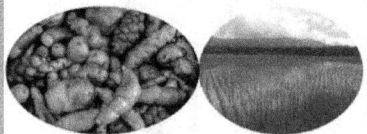

Poetry ... Ekphrasticly Speaking

The Poetry Posse 2022
Gail Weston Shazor * Albert Carasco * Hülya N. Yılmaz
Jackie Davis Allen * Caroline Nazareno * Eliza Segiet
Alicja Maria Kuberska * Teresa E. Gallion * Joe Paire
Kimberly Burnham * Shareef Abdur – Rasheed
Ashok K. Bhargava * Elizabeth Castillo * Swapna Behera
Tezmin Ition Tsai * William S. Peters, Sr.

Now Available
www.innerchildpress.com/the-year-of-the-poet

Inner Child Press Anthologies

The Year of the Poet IX
September 2022

Featured Global Poets
Ngozi Olivia Osuoha * Biswajit Mishra
Sylwia K. Malinowska * Sajid Hussein

Climate Change and Wind and Weather Patterns

Poetry . . . Ekphrasticly Speaking

The Poetry Posse 2022
Gail Weston Shazor * Albert Carasco * Hülya N. Yılmaz
Jackie Davis Allen * Caroline Nazareno * Eliza Segiet
Alicja Maria Kubenska * Teresa E. Gallion * Joe Paire
Kimberly Burnham * Shareef Abdur – Rasheed
Ashok K. Bhargava * Elizabeth Castillo * Swapna Behera
Tezmin Ition Tsai * William S. Peters, Sr

The Year of the Poet IX
October 2022

Featured Global Poets
Andrew Kouroupos * Brenda Mohammed
Carthornia Kouroupos * Faleeha Hassan

Climate Change and Oil and Power

Poetry . . . Ekphrasticly Speaking

The Poetry Posse 2022
Gail Weston Shazor * Albert Carasco * Hülya N. Yılmaz
Jackie Davis Allen * Caroline Nazareno * Eliza Segiet
Alicja Maria Kubenska * Teresa E. Gallion * Joe Paire
Kimberly Burnham * Shareef Abdur – Rasheed
Ashok K. Bhargava * Elizabeth Castillo * Swapna Behera
Tezmin Ition Tsai * William S. Peters, Sr

The Year of the Poet IX
November 2022

Featured Global Poets
Hema Ravi * Shafkat Aziz Hajam
Selma Kopic * Ibrahim Honjo

Climate Change : Time to Act

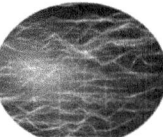

Poetry . . . Ekphrasticly Speaking

The Poetry Posse 2022
Gail Weston Shazor * Albert Carasco * Hülya N. Yılmaz
Jackie Davis Allen * Caroline Nazareno * Eliza Segiet
Alicja Maria Kubenska * Teresa E. Gallion * Joe Paire
Kimberly Burnham * Shareef Abdur – Rasheed
Ashok K. Bhargava * Elizabeth Castillo * Swapna Behera
Tezmin Ition Tsai * William S. Peters, Sr

The Year of the Poet IX
December 2022

Featured Global Poets
Elarbi Abdelfattah * Lorraine Cragg
Neha Bhandarkar * Robert Gibbons

Climate Change Bees, Butterflies and Insect Life

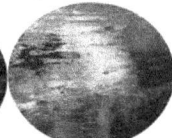

Poetry . . . Ekphrasticly Speaking

The Poetry Posse 2022
Gail Weston Shazor * Albert Carasco * Hülya N. Yılmaz
Jackie Davis Allen * Caroline Nazareno * Eliza Segiet
Alicja Maria Kubenska * Teresa E. Gallion * Joe Paire
Kimberly Burnham * Shareef Abdur – Rasheed
Ashok K. Bhargava * Elizabeth Castillo * Swapna Behera
Tezmin Ition Tsai * William S. Peters, Sr

Now Available
www.innerchildpress.com/the-year-of-the-poet

Inner Child Press Anthologies

The Year of the Poet X
January 2023

Featured Global Poets
JuNe Barefield * Swayam Prashant
Willow Rose * Shabbirhusein K Jamnagerwalla

Children: Difference Makers

Iqbal Masih

The Poetry Posse 2023
Gail Weston Shazor * Albert Carasco * Hülya N. Yılmaz
Jackie Davis Allen * Caroline Nazareno * Kimberly Burnham
Alicja Maria Kuberska * Teresa E. Gallion * Joe Paire
Michelle Joan Barulich * Shareef Abdur – Rasheed
Ashok K. Bhargava * Elizabeth Castillo * Swapna Behera
Tezmin Ition Tsai * Eliza Segiet * William S. Peters, Sr.

The Year of the Poet X
February 2023

Featured Global Poets
Christena Williams * Hilda Graciela Kraft
Francesco Favetta * Dr. H.C. Louise Hudon

Children: Difference Makers

Ruby Bridges

The Poetry Posse 2023
Gail Weston Shazor * Albert Carasco * Hülya N. Yılmaz
Jackie Davis Allen * Caroline Nazareno * Kimberly Burnham
Alicja Maria Kuberska * Teresa E. Gallion * Joe Paire
Michelle Joan Barulich * Shareef Abdur – Rasheed
Ashok K. Bhargava * Elizabeth Castillo * Swapna Behera
Tezmin Ition Tsai * Eliza Segiet * William S. Peters, Sr.

The Year of the Poet X
March 2023

Featured Global Poets
Clarena Martinez Turizo * Binod Dawadi
Til Kumari Sharma * Petrouchka Alexieva

Children: Difference Makers

Yo Yo Ma

The Poetry Posse 2023
Gail Weston Shazor * Albert Carasco * Hülya N. Yılmaz
Jackie Davis Allen * Caroline Nazareno * Kimberly Burnham
Alicja Maria Kuberska * Teresa E. Gallion * Joe Paire
Michelle Joan Barulich * Shareef Abdur – Rasheed
Ashok K. Bhargava * Elizabeth Castillo * Swapna Behera
Tezmin Ition Tsai * Eliza Segiet * William S. Peters, Sr.

The Year of the Poet X
April 2023

Featured Global Poets
Maxwanette A Poetess * Alonzo Gross
Türkan Ergör * Ibrahim Honjo

Children: Difference Makers

Claudette Colvin

The Poetry Posse 2023
Gail Weston Shazor * Albert Carasco * Hülya N. Yılmaz
Jackie Davis Allen * Caroline Nazareno * Kimberly Burnham
Alicja Maria Kuberska * Teresa E. Gallion * Joe Paire
Michelle Joan Barulich * Shareef Abdur – Rasheed
Ashok K. Bhargava * Elizabeth Castillo * Swapna Behera
Tezmin Ition Tsai * Eliza Segiet * William S. Peters, Sr.

Now Available
www.innerchildpress.com/the-year-of-the-poet

Now Available
www.innerchildpress.com/the-year-of-the-poet

Inner Child Press Anthologies

The Year of the Poet X
September 2023

Featured Global Poets
Eftichia Karpadeli * Chinh Nguyen
Nigar Agalarova * Carmela Cueva

Children : Difference Makers

~ Easton LaChappelle ~
The Poetry Posse 2023

Gail Weston Shazor * Albert Carasco * Hülya N. Yılmaz
Jackie Davis Allen * Caroline Nazareno * Kimberly Burnham
Alicja Maria Kuberska * Teresa E. Gallion * Joe Paire
Michelle Joan Barulich * Shareef Abdur – Rasheed
Ashok K. Bhargava * Elizabeth Castillo * Swapna Behera
Tezmin Ition Tsai * Eliza Segiet * William S. Peters, Sr.

The Year of the Poet X
October 2023

Featured Global Poets
CSP Shrivastava * Huniie Parker
Noreen Snyder * Ramkrishna Paul

Children : Difference Makers

~ Malala Yousafzai ~
The Poetry Posse 2023

Gail Weston Shazor * Albert Carasco * Hülya N. Yılmaz
Jackie Davis Allen * Caroline Nazareno * Kimberly Burnham
Alicja Maria Kuberska * Teresa E. Gallion * Joe Paire
Michelle Joan Barulich * Shareef Abdur – Rasheed
Ashok K. Bhargava * Elizabeth Castillo * Swapna Behera
Tezmin Ition Tsai * Eliza Segiet * William S. Peters, Sr.

The Year of the Poet X
November 2023

Featured Global Poets
Ibrahim Honjo * Balachandran Nair
Xanthi Hondrou-Hil * Francesco Favetta

Children : Difference Makers

~ Jean-Michel Basquiat ~
The Poetry Posse 2023

Gail Weston Shazor * Albert Carasco * Hülya N. Yılmaz
Jackie Davis Allen * Caroline Nazareno * Kimberly Burnham
Alicja Maria Kuberska * Teresa E. Gallion * Joe Paire
Michelle Joan Barulich * Shareef Abdur – Rasheed
Ashok K. Bhargava * Elizabeth Castillo * Swapna Behera
Tezmin Ition Tsai * Eliza Segiet * William S. Peters, Sr.

The Year of the Poet X
December 2023

Featured Global Poets
Caroline Laurent Turunc * Neha Bhandarkar
Shafkat Aziz Hajam * Elarbi Abdelfattah

Children : Difference Makers

~ Melati and Isabel Wijsen ~
The Poetry Posse 2023

Gail Weston Shazor * Albert Carasco * Hülya N. Yılmaz
Jackie Davis Allen * Caroline Nazareno * Kimberly Burnham
Alicja Maria Kuberska * Teresa E. Gallion * Joe Paire
Michelle Joan Barulich * Shareef Abdur – Rasheed
Ashok K. Bhargava * Elizabeth Castillo * Swapna Behera
Tezmin Ition Tsai * Eliza Segiet * William S. Peters, Sr.

Now Available
www.innerchildpress.com/the-year-of-the-poet

Inner Child Press Anthologies

The Year of the Poet XI
January 2024

Featured Global Poets
Til Kumari Sharma * Shafkat Aziz Hajam
Daniela Marian * Eleni Vassiliou – Asteroskon

Renowned Poets

~ Phyllis Wheatley ~
The Poetry Posse 2024
Gail Weston Shazor * Albert Carasco * Hülya N. Yılmaz
Jackie Davis Allen * Caroline Nazareno * Mutawaf Shaheed
Alicja Maria Kuberska * Teresa E. Gallion * Noreen Snyder
Michelle Joan Barulich * Shareef Abdur – Rasheed
Ashok K. Bhargava * Elizabeth Castillo * Swapna Behera
Tezmin Ition Tsai * Eliza Segiet * William S. Peters, Sr.

The Year of the Poet XI
February 2024

Featured Global Poets
Caroline Laurent Turunç * Julio Pavanetti
Lidia Chiarelli * Lina Buividavičiūtė

Renowned Poets

~ Omar Khayyam ~
The Poetry Posse 2024
Gail Weston Shazor * Albert Carasco * Hülya N. Yılmaz
Jackie Davis Allen * Caroline Nazareno * Mutawaf Shaheed
Alicja Maria Kuberska * Teresa E. Gallion * Noreen Snyder
Michelle Joan Barulich * Shareef Abdur – Rasheed
Ashok K. Bhargava * Elizabeth Castillo * Swapna Behera
Tezmin Ition Tsai * Eliza Segiet * William S. Peters, Sr.

The Year of the Poet XI
March 2024

Featured Global Poets
Francesco Favetta * Jagjit Singh Zandu
Carmela Núñez Yukimura Peruana * Michael Lee Johnson

Renowned Poets

~ Nâzım Hikmet ~
The Poetry Posse 2024
Gail Weston Shazor * Albert Carasco * Hülya N. Yılmaz
Jackie Davis Allen * Caroline Nazareno * Mutawaf Shaheed
Alicja Maria Kuberska * Teresa E. Gallion * Noreen Snyder
Michelle Joan Barulich * Shareef Abdur – Rasheed
Ashok K. Bhargava * Elizabeth Castillo * Swapna Behera
Tezmin Ition Tsai * Eliza Segiet * William S. Peters, Sr.

The Year of the Poet XI
April 2024

Featured Global Poets
Hassanal Abdullah * Johny Takkedasila
Rajashree Mohapatra * Shirley Smothers

Renowned Poets

~ William Butler Yeats ~
The Poetry Posse 2024
Gail Weston Shazor * Albert Carasco * Hülya N. Yılmaz
Jackie Davis Allen * Caroline Nazareno * Mutawaf Shaheed
Alicja Maria Kuberska * Teresa E. Gallion * Noreen Snyder
Michelle Joan Barulich * Shareef Abdur – Rasheed
Ashok K. Bhargava * Elizabeth Castillo * Swapna Behera
Tezmin Ition Tsai * Eliza Segiet * William S. Peters, Sr.

Now Available
www.innerchildpress.com/the-year-of-the-poet

Inner Child Press Anthologies

The Year of the Poet XI
May 2024

Featured Global Poets
Binod Dawadi * Petros Kyriakou Veloudas
Rayees Ahmad Kumar * Solomon C Jatta

Renowned Poets

~ Makhanlal Chaturvedi ~
The Poetry Posse 2024

Gail Weston Shazor * Albert Carasco * Hülya N. Yılmaz
Jackie Davis Allen * Caroline Nazareno * Mutawaf Shaheed
Alicja Maria Kuberska * Teresa E. Gallion * Noreen Snyder
Michelle Joan Barulich * Shareef Abdur – Rasheed
Ashok K. Bhargava * Elizabeth Castillo * Swapna Behera
Tezmin Ition Tsai * Eliza Segiet * William S. Peters, Sr.

The Year of the Poet XI
June 2024

Featured Global Poets
C. S. P Shrivastava * Maria Evelyn Quilla Soleta
Moulay Cherif Chebihi Hassani * Swayam Prashant

Renowned Poets

~ Langston Hughs ~
The Poetry Posse 2024

Gail Weston Shazor * Albert Carasco * Hülya N. Yılmaz
Jackie Davis Allen * Caroline Nazareno * Mutawaf Shaheed
Alicja Maria Kuberska * Teresa E. Gallion * Noreen Snyder
Michelle Joan Barulich * Shareef Abdur – Rasheed
Ashok K. Bhargava * Elizabeth Castillo * Swapna Behera
Tezmin Ition Tsai * Eliza Segiet * William S. Peters, Sr.

The Year of the Poet XI
July 2024

Featured Global Poets
Barbara Gaiardoni * Bharati Nayak
Errol Bean * Michael Lee Johnson

Renowned Poets

~ Pablo Neruda ~
The Poetry Posse 2024

Gail Weston Shazor * Albert Carasco * Hülya N. Yılmaz
Jackie Davis Allen * Caroline Nazareno * Mutawaf Shaheed
Alicja Maria Kuberska * Teresa E. Gallion * Noreen Snyder
Michelle Joan Barulich * Shareef Abdur – Rasheed
Ashok K. Bhargava * Elizabeth Castillo * Swapna Behera
Tezmin Ition Tsai * Eliza Segiet * William S. Peters, Sr.

The Year of the Poet XI
August 2024

Featured Global Poets
Ibrahim Honjo * Khalice Jade
Irma Kurti * Mennadi Farah

Renowned Poets

~ Li Bai ~
The Poetry Posse 2024

Gail Weston Shazor * Albert Carasco * Hülya N. Yılmaz
Jackie Davis Allen * Caroline Nazareno * Mutawaf Shaheed
Alicja Maria Kuberska * Teresa E. Gallion * Noreen Snyder
Michelle Joan Barulich * Shareef Abdur – Rasheed
Ashok K. Bhargava * Elizabeth Castillo * Swapna Behera
Tezmin Ition Tsai * Eliza Segiet * William S. Peters, Sr.

Now Available
www.innerchildpress.com/the-year-of-the-poet

Inner Child Press Anthologies

The Year of the Poet XI
September 2024

Featured Global Poets
Ngozi Olivia Osuoha * Teodozja Świderska
Chinh Nguyen * Awatef El Idrissi Boukhris

Renowned Poets

~ William Ernest Henley ~
The Poetry Posse 2024
Gail Weston Shazor * Albert Carasco * Hülya N. Yılmaz
Jackie Davis Allen * Caroline Nazareno * Mutawaf Shaheed
Alicja Maria Kuberska * Teresa E. Gallion * Noreen Snyder
Michelle Joan Barulich * Shareef Abdur – Rasheed
Ashok K. Bhargava * Elizabeth Castillo * Swapna Behera
Tzemin Ition Tsai * Eliza Segiet * William S. Peters, Sr.

The Year of the Poet XI
October 2024

Featured Global Poets
Deepak Kumar Dey * Shallal 'Anouz
Adnan Al-Sayegh * Taghrid Bou Merhi

Renowned Poets

~ Adam Mickiewicz ~
The Poetry Posse 2024
Gail Weston Shazor * Albert Carasco * Hülya N. Yılmaz
Jackie Davis Allen * Caroline Nazareno * Mutawaf Shaheed
Alicja Maria Kuberska * Teresa E. Gallion * Noreen Snyder
Michelle Joan Barulich * Shareef Abdur – Rasheed
Ashok K. Bhargava * Elizabeth Castillo * Swapna Behera
Tzemin Ition Tsai * Eliza Segiet * William S. Peters, Sr.

The Year of the Poet XI
November 2024

Featured Global Poets
Abraham Tawiah Tei * Neha Bhandarkar
Zaneta Varnado Johns * Haseena Bnaiyan

Renowned Poets

~ Wole Soyinka ~
The Poetry Posse 2024
Gail Weston Shazor * Albert Carasco * Hülya N. Yılmaz
Jackie Davis Allen * Caroline Nazareno * Mutawaf Shaheed
Alicja Maria Kuberska * Teresa E. Gallion * Noreen Snyder
Michelle Joan Barulich * Shareef Abdur – Rasheed
Ashok K. Bhargava * Elizabeth Castillo * Swapna Behera
Tzemin Ition Tsai * Eliza Segiet * William S. Peters, Sr.

The Year of the Poet XI
December 2024

Featured Global Poets
Kapardeli Eftichia * Irena Jovanović
Sudipta Mishra * Til Kumari Sharma

Renowned Poets

~ Imru' al-Qais ~
The Poetry Posse 2024
Gail Weston Shazor * Albert Carasco * Hülya N. Yılmaz
Jackie Davis Allen * Caroline Nazareno * Mutawaf Shaheed
Alicja Maria Kuberska * Teresa E. Gallion * Noreen Snyder
Michelle Joan Barulich * Shareef Abdur – Rasheed * Swapna Behera
Ashok K. Bhargava * Elizabeth Castillo * Kimberly Burnham
Tzemin Ition Tsai * Eliza Segiet * William S. Peters, Sr.

Now Available
www.innerchildpress.com/the-year-of-the-poet

Inner Child Press Anthologies

The Year of the Poet XII
January 2025

Featured Global Poets

Khalice Jade * Til Kumari Sharma
Sushant Thapa * Orbindu Ganga

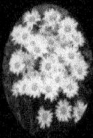 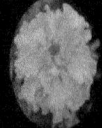 

Innocence	Joy	Longing
Daisy	Marigold	Camellia

The Poetry Posse 2025

Gail Weston Shazor * Albert Carassco * Hülya N. Yılmaz
Jackie Davis Allen * Caroline Nazareno * Mutawaf Shaheed
Alicja Maria Kuberska * Teresa E. Gallion * Noreen Snyder
Shareef Abdur – Rasheed * Swapna Behera * Eliza Segiet
Ashok K. Bhargava * Elizabeth Castillo * Kimberly Burnham
Tzemin Ition Tsai * William S. Peters, Sr.

The Year of the Poet XII
February 2025

Featured Global Poets

Shafkat Aziz Hajam * Frosina Tasevska
Muhammad Gaddafi Masoud * Karen Morrison

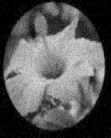 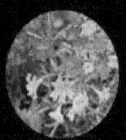 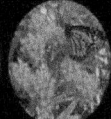

Curiosity	Fear	Lonlines
Hibiscus	Minulus	Butterfly Weed

The Poetry Posse 2025

Gail Weston Shazor * Albert Carassco * Hülya N. Yılmaz
Jackie Davis Allen * Caroline Nazareno * Mutawaf Shaheed
Alicja Maria Kuberska * Teresa E. Gallion * Noreen Snyder
Shareef Abdur – Rasheed * Swapna Behera * Eliza Segiet
Ashok K. Bhargava * Elizabeth Castillo * Kimberly Burnham
Tzemin Ition Tsai * William S. Peters, Sr.

The Year of the Poet XII
March 2025

Featured Global Poets

Deepak Kumar Dey * Binod Dawadi
Faleeha Hassan * Kapardeli Eftichia

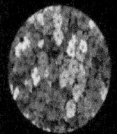  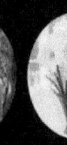

Frustration	Sorrow	Detrmination
Petunias	Purple Hyacinth	Amaryllis

The Poetry Posse 2025

Gail Weston Shazor * Albert Carassco * Hülya N. Yılmaz
Jackie Davis Allen * Caroline Nazareno * Mutawaf Shaheed
Alicja Maria Kuberska * Teresa E. Gallion * Noreen Snyder
Shareef Abdur – Rasheed * Swapna Behera * Eliza Segiet
Ashok K. Bhargava * Elizabeth Castillo * Kimberly Burnham
Tzemin Ition Tsai * William S. Peters, Sr.

The Year of the Poet XII
April 2025

Featured Global Poets

Gopal Sinha * Taghrid Bou Merhi
Irma Kurti * Marlon Salem Gruezo

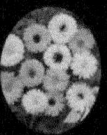  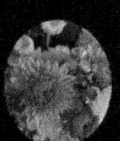

Resilience	Self Doubt	Grief
Calendula	Centaury	Chrysanthemums

The Poetry Posse 2025

Gail Weston Shazor * Albert Carassco * Hülya N. Yılmaz
Jackie Davis Allen * Caroline Nazareno * Mutawaf Shaheed
Alicja Maria Kuberska * Teresa E. Gallion * Noreen Snyder
Shareef Abdur – Rasheed * Swapna Behera * Eliza Segiet
Ashok K. Bhargava * Elizabeth Castillo * Kimberly Burnham
Tzemin Ition Tsai * William S. Peters, Sr.

Now Available
www.innerchildpress.com/the-year-of-the-poet

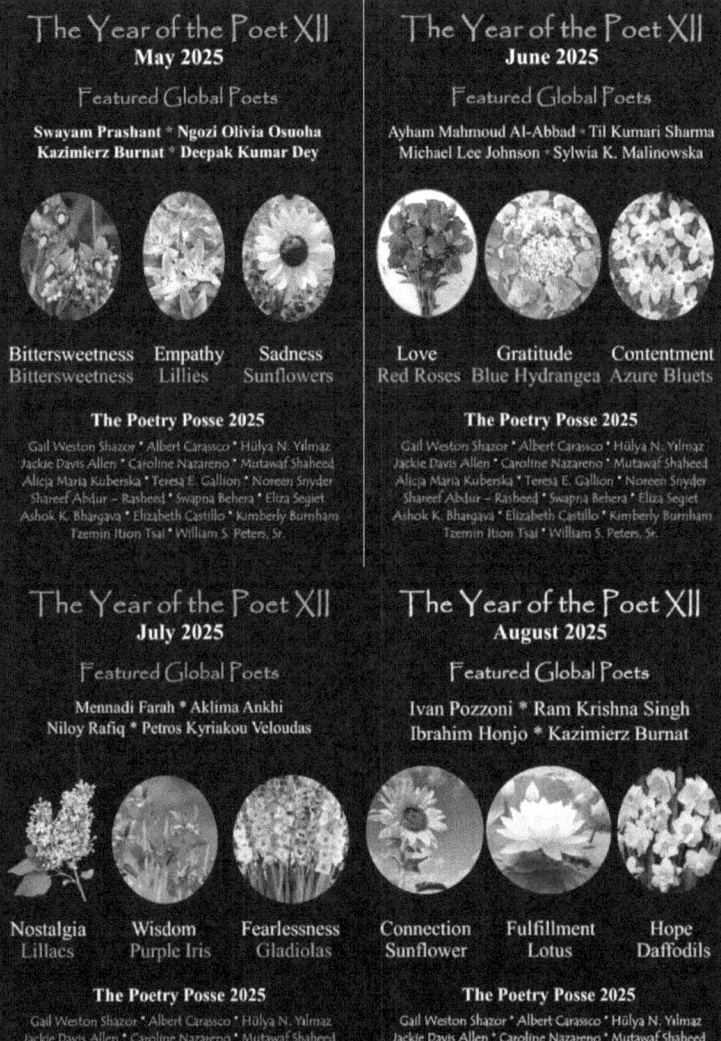

and there is much, much more !

visit . . .

www.innerchildpress.com/anthologies-sales-special.php

Also check out our Authors and all the wonderful Books Available at :

www.innerchildpress.com/authors-pages

Inner Child Press Anthologies

Now Available

www.worldhealingworldpeacepoetry.com

Inner Child Press Anthologies

Now Available

www.worldhealingworldpeacepoetry.com

Inner Child Press Anthologies

Now Available

www.worldhealingworldpeacepoetry.com

Inner Child Press Anthologies

Now Available

www.worldhealingworldpeacepoetry.com

World Healing World Peace

2012, 2014, 2016, 2018, 2020, 2022, 2024

Now Available

www.worldhealingworldpeacepoetry.com

Inner Child Press International

'building bridges of cultural understanding'

Meet the Board of Directors

William S. Peters, Sr.
Chair Person
Founder
Inner Child Enterprises
Inner Child Press

Hülya N Yılmaz
Director
Editing Services
Co-Chair Person

Fahredin B. Shehu
Director
Cultural Affairs

Elizabeth E. Castillo
Director
Recording Secretary

De'Andre Hawthorne
Director
Performance Poetry

Gail Weston Shazor
Director
Anthologies

Kimberly Burnham
Director
Cultural Ambassador
Pacific Northwest
USA

Ashok K. Bhargava
Director
WIN Awards

Deborah Smart
Director
Publicity
Marketing

Khalice Jade
Director
Translation
Services

www.innerchildpress.com

This Anthological Publication
is underwritten solely by

Inner Child Press International

Inner Child Press is a Publishing Company Founded and Operated by Writers. Our personal publishing experiences provides us an intimate understanding of the sometimes daunting challenges Writers, New and Seasoned may face in the Business of Publishing and Marketing their Creative "Written Work".

For more Information

Inner Child Press International

www.innerchildpress.com

'building bridges of cultural understanding'   www.innerchildpress.com
202 Wiltree Court, State College, Pennsylvania 16801

This is our world . . .

~ fini ~

www.ingramcontent.com/pod-product-compliance
Lightning Source LLC
LaVergne TN
LVHW051042080426
835508LV00019B/1653